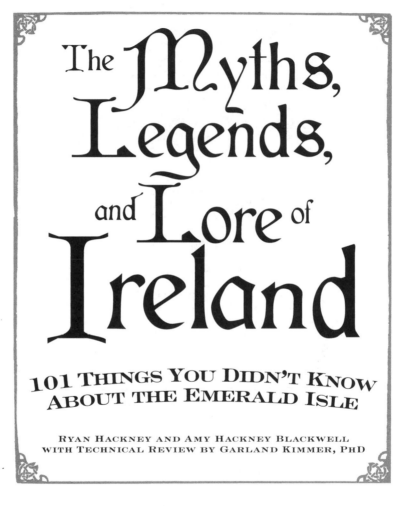

# The Myths, Legends, and Lore of Ireland

## 101 Things You Didn't Know About the Emerald Isle

RYAN HACKNEY AND AMY HACKNEY BLACKWELL
WITH TECHNICAL REVIEW BY GARLAND KIMMER, PhD

Adamsmedia

AVON, MASSACHUSETTS

Published by
Adams Media, a division of F+W Media, Inc.
57 Littlefield Street, Avon, MA 02322. U.S.A.
*www.adamsmedia.com*

ISBN 10: 1-4405-0607-8
ISBN 13: 978-1-4405-0607-9
eISBN 10: 1-4405-0924-7
eISBN 13: 978-1-4405-0924-7

Printed in the United States of America.

10   9   8   7   6   5   4   3   2   1

**Library of Congress Cataloging-in-Publication Data**
is available from the publisher.

Many of the designations used by manufacturers and sellers to distinguish their product are claimed as trademarks. Where those designations appear in this book and Adams Media was aware of a trademark claim, the designations have been printed with initial capital letters.

Previously published as *101 Things You Didn't Know about Irish History*, by Ryan Hackney and Amy Hackney Blackwell with Technical Review by Garland Kimmer, PhD, copyright © 2007 by F+W Media, Inc., ISBN 10: 1-59869-323-9, ISBN 13: 978-1-59869-323-2.

Contains material adapted and abridged from *The Everything® Irish History and Heritage Book* by Ryan Hackney and Amy Hackney Blackwell, copyright © 2004 by F+W Media, Inc., ISBN 10: 1-58062-980-6, ISBN 13: 978-1-58062-980-5.

Irish flag art © istockphoto / Magcom

*This book is available at quantity discounts for bulk purchases.*
*For information, please call 1-800-289-0963.*

# Contents

## ♣ PART TWO: THE ARRIVAL OF CHRISTIANITY (AND THE BRITISH, TOO!)

## ♣ PART THREE: PRESERVING IRISH CULTURE AND HISTORY

## ♣ PART FOUR: EMIGRATION TO MODERN LIFE

# Introduction

Ireland is an island that transcends both its geographical and political boundaries. This transcendence has not occurred because of either a powerful military or economic presence. It has, in fact, occurred despite the notable lack of either. Instead, Ireland can be found on every continent through the memories, stories, and dreams of the immigrants, exiles, and friends who treasure Irish culture. Recent population statistics show just over 4.2 million citizens in the Republic of Ireland, while counting the numbers of Irish expatriates presents a much larger, more complex problem. Numbers range as high as 80 million Irish émigrés, a figure that suggests that Irishness exists as prominently metaphorically and spiritually as literally.

Perhaps more than any other culture, Ireland lives with the fundamental tension between its past and its present, between tradition and change, in the foreground of its everyday existence. The Ireland of today is simultaneously the same and very different from the Ireland of my first visit in 1987. That summer, I spent time in Dublin, Sligo, and Galway. I was making a tour of Ireland's recent literary past, and it was easy to believe that Ireland's past was more alive and vibrant than its present.

Just a couple of years later, Mary Robinson became Ireland's seventh president. If that office has traditionally been symbolic, Robinson turned both the symbolism and the role of the office on end. Her tenure underscores Ireland's seemingly split personality. It is a culture that values tradition and history yet is not afraid to adapt and develop. Aside from being the first elected President to not have the support of Fianna Fáil and Ireland's first female President, Robinson shifted the ground rules for the office—which you'll learn about in this book. Moreover, she took Ireland onto the international stage more powerfully than ever before by becoming the UN's High Commissioner for Human Rights. She advocated powerfully for human rights out of the Ireland's historic relationships with its more powerful neighbors.

In Irish letters, this difficult and at times diffident relationship between past and present lingered throughout the twentieth century. James Joyce worried that this was the case when he described Dublin as the center of Ireland's paralysis in a letter to his publisher. Joyce found his vision of Dublin at a remove, writing in France and Switzerland to create in Dublin the quintessential setting for exploring the tensions between group and individual identity. This thematic tension dates back to early Celtic culture in Ireland, where existence outside the tribe was unthinkable.

Like Joyce, both W. B. Yeats and Seamus Heaney are intimately aware of their interactions with the historical (or perhaps prehistorical) role of the Irish poet. Poets possessed a power and prestige that allowed them to exist outside of the tribe and to move freely from place to place. Yeats's term as a senator in the 1920s hints at the prestige attached to men of letters that persisted into the twentieth century and beyond. Heaney's self-described status as an "artful voyeur" in "Punishment," a poem that works as allegory for the Troubles in the North, serves as a reminder of the poet's historical role as both chronicler of and outsider to the tribe.

The constant awareness of how Ireland's epic, mythological past maintains itself into the present comes sharply into focus in the following pages: *The Myths, Legends, and Lore of Ireland* can give you a start to learning about Irish history and heritage, but there is so much more to learn. This book brings you into Ireland thousands of years ago and leaves you in the present.

—*Garland Kimmer, PhD*

# Part 1

# Prehistory and Mythology of Ancient Ireland

Ireland is an island with a past. People lived there for millennia before anyone started recording history, and they left their mark on the landscape—standing stones, odd-looking structures, great mounds of earth. The presence of so many prehistoric remains, a lot of which are pre-Celtic, ties Ireland's past to its present. Celtic culture is everywhere in Ireland, from the stone-crosses in the countryside to patterns knit into wool sweaters. The influence of the Celts is remarkable, considering how little is actually known about them.

# 1} The Earliest Inhabitants

Compared with the European mainland, Ireland hasn't been inhabited for very long. Africa, the Middle East, and central Europe have all housed humans for hundreds of thousands of years, and there is evidence of humans in England going back at least 250,000 years. But it was only about 9,000 years ago that anyone ventured to the Emerald Isle. Why was this? One word: ice.

Ireland was covered with ice for a very long time. It had few plants, and the only animals who lived there were creatures that preferred snow and ice, such as reindeer, woolly mammoths, and the spectacular Irish giant deer. The temperature fluctuated, but mostly just in variations on the same theme of cold.

About 13,000 years ago, the ice finally started to recede, and Ireland warmed up. This was bad for some of the larger mammals, which became extinct, but it was good for smaller creatures and plants. No one knows for sure how Ireland's wildlife got there; maybe it floated across the Irish Sea, or maybe there was a temporary bridge of land between Ireland and what is now called England. In any case, by about 5000 B.C.E. Ireland was covered with forests and full of wild beasts.

## 2 } Mesolithic Age and the First Farmers

These conditions made Ireland even more attractive to humans. The early settlers did not leave behind much information about themselves. Mostly, archaeologists have found stone tools—things like axes, knives, and scrapers. People used these tools to chop plants or skin animals. Ireland is full of these stone tools, many of which have been picked up by amateur collectors.

Flint is one of the best stones for tool making, and the best flint in Ireland is in the northeastern corner. And that's where most of Ireland's stone tools have been found—in Antrim, Down, and the Strangford Lough area. One of the best Mesolithic sites is Mount Sandel in County Derry, where archaeologists have found the remains of several little dome-shaped huts, built there between 7010 and 6490 B.C.E. Here, people lived, huddled around their fires, eating nuts, berries, pigs, birds, and fish.

The Mesolithic Period, also known as the Middle Stone Age, lasted for several thousand years. Stone technology did not change much during this time. People lived a fairly migratory existence, moving around in pursuit of plants and animals. Around 4000 B.C.E., things changed. People began to grow food and make pottery. They cleared forests for their fields and built more permanent settlements. Archaeologists call this new period the Neolithic Period, or New Stone Age.

It's possible that the Mesolithic Irish developed this new technology on their own, but it's more likely that these changes came over the ocean with new immigrants. The newcomers either conquered the people already living there, or, more likely, they just assimilated them, intermarrying and sharing techniques for making tools and growing food. This assimilation worked in both directions. It brought new things while keeping the old, and this layering was vital to Irish culture later.

Neolithic people built their houses out of wood. These houses have mostly decayed, but their foundations are still visible. Archaeologists have also found lots of new tools for grinding wheat and a huge number of polished stone axes made from a stone called porcellanite.

# 3 } Legends and Archaeology

Stone Age people built a lot of tombs or tomblike structures out of gigantic rocks covered with mounds of earth; this building technique makes the tombs look like big, grassy mushrooms from the outside. These ancient tombs continue to intrigue people today; there are so many of them all over the landscape, they're hard to miss.

The megalithic tombs were probably constructed shortly before the arrival of the Celts, who called them fairy mounds and believed that the spirits of ancient people—bold heroes and brave maidens—lived there. The Celtic creator gods, the Tuatha Dé Danann, were known to be fabulously good at building things, and perhaps it was they who constructed the tombs dotting the countryside.

Eventually, the spirits inhabiting the fairy mounds transformed into the little people of later Irish legends—leprechauns and fairies and brownies, whose spirits are said to haunt the land.

Many of these tombs are called passage tombs because they contain passages leading to burial chambers underneath the mound. The walls of the passage and chamber are made of rock that is often elaborately carved.

Court tombs, or *cairns*, have an open, roofless courtyard in front leading into two, three, or four chambers at back. Archaeologists have found human remains in them but think that they might originally have been built as temples. They tend to be evenly distributed about 3 miles apart instead of clustered like graves; generally structures that are spaced like that are places of worship, but there's no way to tell for sure how people used them.

Wedge tombs also occur primarily in the northern part of Ireland. These tombs have stone walls and roofs; the roof gets lower and the passage narrower as one goes into the tomb, hence the name wedge. Most of them face west or southwest, toward the setting sun.

Wedge tombs are numerous; there are about 500 of them all over the northern part of the country, although some can be found on Ireland's eastern coastline. The ones that have been excavated contain human remains, and some contain pottery, which suggests that they were made toward the end of the Neolithic period. *Labbacallee* ("Hag's Bed"), in

County Cork, is an excellent wedge tomb. It got its strange name because it contained the skeleton of a headless woman when it was first opened.

Portal tombs, also called dolmens, consist of several large upright stones topped by a giant capstone. Putting these rocks in place must have been a stupendous effort—some capstones weigh as much as 100 tons. These dolmens were originally surrounded by mounds of earth, and people were buried inside them. A giant dolmen at Poulnabrone, County Clare, had more than twenty people buried in it over a 600-year period; this might mean that only royalty was buried there. There are dolmens all over Ireland, as well as in Wales and Cornwall. The Kilclooney More dolmen in County Donegal is particularly cool—its capstone is almost 14 feet long.

Some of the most spectacular archaeological sites from the Neolithic period are in the Boyne Valley in County Meath. These sites are called *Brú na Bóinne*, which means "Boyne Palace." They consist of large stone tombs built around 3200 B.C.E., several centuries before the great pyramids of Egypt. The three main components of this site are Newgrange, Knowth, and Dowth.

People have known about these tombs for centuries; Vikings plundered them, while Victorians hunted treasures there and carved their initials on the walls. The sites gradually deteriorated and were even quarried at one point. The Republic of Ireland has become very interested in its history, however, and consequently, the tombs have been extensively restored.

The tombs at Newgrange are built inside a huge, grassy mound of earth. The stones at the entrance and some of the stones holding the tomb together are elaborately carved with spirals.

These stones are not local; some of them came from Wicklow, 50 miles away, and others from Northern Ireland. This indicates that whoever built them was very organized—it's not easy to assemble the manpower to transport big rocks over that many miles. The tomb might have been surrounded by a ring of giant stones, though only twelve of these now remain. It sounds a little like Stonehenge, something to which the tomb has been compared.

Inside the mound is a long passageway leading to a subterranean burial chamber. Inside this chamber are three recesses for holding remains. The front door of Newgrange is a solar observatory extraordinaire. When the tomb was first excavated by experts, archaeologists found the remains of at least three cremated bodies and some human bones. Offerings of jewelry were probably once there as well, but these were stolen long ago.

No one knows exactly why these mounds were built. They might have been burial places for kings; ancient legends certainly suggest that as a possibility. Or they might have served as calendars. Many megalithic sites are constructed to catch the sun at particular times of the year, and they are astonishingly accurate.

Newgrange is the best-known example of this. Every year during the winter solstice (December 19–23), the rising sun shines through a slit over the entrance and lights up the burial chamber for seventeen minutes. At the time the tomb was built, the sunlight would have shone directly onto a spiral design carved into the wall.

Similar solar phenomena happen at other megalithic sites. The light of the setting sun at winter solstice illuminates one of the chambers inside Dowth. At Knowth, the eastern passage seems to have been designed to catch the rising sun of the spring and autumn equinoxes, while the western passage might have caught the setting sun on those same days.

The tombs at Brú na Bóinne are an extremely popular tourist destination. The tour of Newgrange features a fake winter solstice sunrise, so that visitors can see how the sun illuminates the chamber. But don't get your hopes up about seeing the real thing; admission to the Newgrange chamber for the winter solstice sunrise is by lottery. Fifty names were chosen from more than 25,000 for the 2010 event.

The River Boyne, which flows past these mound tombs, has long been very important spiritually to the Irish people. Legend says that the first occupant of Newgrange was named Elcmar. His wife was Boann, the spirit of the river.

# 4 ⸱ The Bronze Age

Around 2400 B.C.E., life in Ireland began to change again. People started making tools out of metal instead of stone. These metalworkers might have been a new wave of immigrants bringing their craft with them, or they might have been the folks already in Ireland. Whoever they were, their metal tools were much better than stone ones.

This period is called the Bronze Age because most of these tools were made of bronze, an alloy made of copper and tin mixed together. Ireland has tons of copper, and archaeologists have found traces of many copper mines. Tin is harder to get; people might have imported it from England or possibly from Brittany in France.

Smiths shaped bronze into all kinds of objects, including axes, spearheads, and jewelry. They decorated some of these with triangles and zigzags, which gives the impression that these objects might have been more for show than for use.

Ireland also had a fair amount of gold hidden in its hills, and Bronze Age smiths used it to make some spectacular jewelry—thick bracelets and necklaces called torques, fancy hairpins, and half-moon-shaped trinkets that they probably hung around their necks. They also made disks of thin sheets of gold with hammered decoration; these are called sun discs, and people might have worn them as jewelry, too. Examples of these jewels can be seen at the National Museum of Ireland in Dublin.

# 5 } Iron Comes to Ireland

The Bronze Age in Ireland ended around 800 B.C.E. Bronze tools disappeared and iron ones took their place. This must have been the result of increased contact with Britain, which was in closer contact with the rest of Europe, where iron was all the rage.

Early iron wasn't superior to bronze—in the days before steel was invented, iron was ugly and of poor quality. But iron ore was readily available almost everywhere, and supplies of tin, necessary for making bronze, were not. And so blacksmiths stuck with it and gradually got better at using it.

The Iron Age didn't start all at once. People gradually started using more iron and less bronze. In the late eighth century B.C.E., iron was prevalent on the Continent, and a century later it was widespread in Britain. Irish smiths at this time were working with both metals, producing distinctive swords and other artifacts.

The iron-using people also had horses. Archaeologists have found many bits for bridles and other tidbits of equestrian gear. They have also unearthed miles and miles of wooden tracks beneath the bogs, paths made of giant oak planks laid side by side; these would have made transporting goods by horse and cart much easier than dragging them through Ireland's soft soil.

The advent of iron is often associated with the arrival of the people called the Celts. By 300 B.C.E., the Celtic artistic style was thoroughly established in the northern part of Ireland. The Celts spread their culture and language throughout Ireland over the next several centuries, mixing their beliefs with Christianity and resisting foreign assailants as long as they could.

# 6{ Who Were the Celts and Kings?

It's hard to say anything conclusive about the Celts, because they didn't record their history themselves. They couldn't write (with one minor exception, which we discuss later in this section). Most everything we know about them today comes from either the archaeological evidence or the accounts of Roman visitors that were transcribed by medieval Christians. This means that all of our written records on the Celts were filtered through two sets of biases: the Romans, who looked on them as an alien culture that needed to be conquered, and the Christians, who thought the Celts were pagans who hadn't seen the truth of Christ. And modern observers have all kinds of opinions that color their views.

According to classical writers, most of the people who lived in northwestern and central Europe were Celts—*keltoi* in Greek. Ancient writers knew of Celtic people in Spain, France, Germany, Switzerland, and modern Austria. Celts were hard to miss, because they were violent; various Celtic peoples started attacking Greek and Roman settlements around 400 B.C.E. and kept attacking as long as there was loot to be had.

The ancients thought the Celts had originated in Switzerland and spread out from there. They envisioned the Celts as a warrior people who marched from country to country, attacking civilized people and settling wherever they conquered. Modern scholars think it more likely that the Celtic language and culture spread from group to group through trade, though there was certainly some fighting involved, too. This Celtic culture moved over the Continent and into the British Isles until, by the fourth century B.C.E., most of the people in northwestern Europe and Britain were members of this cultural group.

Historians have long imagined ancient history as a series of peoples taking over land from one another. When they envisioned the Celts, they saw warriors who came marauding over the countryside, laying waste and taking over local wealth. While there is some truth to this picture, it seems that cultural spread was actually a much gentler process most of the time.

The people who became known as the Irish were probably a mix of indigenous peoples—remember the folks who built those mounds and tombs?—and immigrants who brought new language and technology with them. The newcomers entered Irish society by marrying the natives, although there was probably some violence as well. Irish legend gives the impression that a bunch of warriors arrived several centuries before Christ and established chiefdoms for themselves all over the country. The Celtic languages became predominant either through military domination or because they were more prestigious for other reasons. However it happened, by the time the Romans arrived, the Irish people were speaking Celtic languages.

# 7 } Gaelic and Indo-European Languages

Although Celtic languages and cultures were similar to one another, they were by no means identical; there were a vast number of physical types and cultural traditions that fell under the heading Celtic. The Celts who settled in France became known as Gauls. The ones in Britain became the Bretons and the Welsh.

The Celts who arrived in Ireland sometime around 350 B.C.E. didn't belong to the same group as the Celts in Britain. Most of the ancestors of the Irish Celts came from Spain. Language is the clue to their origin.

Linguists classify languages into families of related tongues. Almost all European languages—including French, German, English, and Irish—are grouped into a giant family called Indo-European, which also includes such ancient languages as Latin, Sanskrit, and Hittite. Finnish, Hungarian, Basque, and Estonian are exceptions—they are European but do not belong in the Indo-European group. All Indo-European languages show basic similarities in vocabulary and grammar that suggest they might have come from a single language—proto-Indo-European.

It is believed that proto-Indo-European may have been spoken many thousands of years ago somewhere north of the Black Sea. The people who spoke this language apparently traveled extensively in Central Asia and Europe, and forms of their language took root throughout these regions. One of the major language groups to develop this way was the Celtic family.

There were many Celtic languages, and the Irish language is just one of them. Irish comes from the Celtic branch called *Goidelic,* which also includes Scots Gaelic. The term *Goidelic* comes from the Irish Celts' name for themselves, *Goídil,* which gives us the modern word Gaelic. Irish is not very closely related to the languages spoken nearby, particularly Welsh and Breton (spoken in Brittany, France), but instead had its roots in Spain; hence, scholars think the ancestors of the Irish came from Spain.

# 8 } Celtic Ireland

People studying Ireland actually have an advantage over those scrutinizing Celts from other lands, because a number of ancient Irish stories and other writings survive. The Celts didn't write these things down themselves; they transmitted their culture orally. But centuries later, medieval monks, in their zeal to preserve stories of the oral tradition in written form, wrote down a bunch of ancient Celtic legends and books of laws, and these offer the modern reader a unique glimpse into ancient Irish life. This life seems to have included heroes, feasts, cattle raids, and love affairs.

The land was divided into five areas:

1. **Leinster**—the southeast
2. **Meath**—the middle

3. **Connacht**—the west
4. **Ulster**—the north
5. **Munster**—the southwest

Each of these provinces was divided into 100 or so smaller sections called *tuatha*, or tribes, each governed by its own chieftain, called a *rí*. People were divided into clans, and several clans made up a tribe. Ordinary people swore allegiance to their local king. Sometimes one man would rise above all the others and become high king of all Ireland.

## 9§ Wild and Crazy Heroes

The Irish were obsessed with war, weapons, and heroics. If their poetry is any indication, they spent most of their time at war with one another, stealing cattle, and feasting on pork.

The Celts scared the Romans and other "civilized" contemporary observers. When they went into battle, they would strip naked and dash at their enemies dressed in nothing but sandals and their fancy necklaces. They howled as if possessed by demons, their shrieks augmented by loud bagpipes.

Some warriors would be so overcome by battle-frenzy that their very appearance changed. They called this transformation the warp-spasm. The *Táin Bó Cuailnge* has an excellent description of the hero Cuchulain (or Cú

Chulainn) undergoing this phenomenon, which involved most of his body turning itself inside out and fire and blood shooting out of his head, after which he killed hundreds of enemy warriors and walked away unscathed.

Cattle and metal treasure were the main forms of wealth in ancient Ireland—metal because it was rare, and cattle because they were useful. Cattle provided milk to drink and to make into cheese, and hide and meat after they were dead. If a king demanded tribute from his subjects, it would probably be in the form of cattle—in fact, a wealthy farmer was called a *bóiare*, or "lord of cows." In the famous poem *Táin Bó Cuailnge*, a major war starts because Queen Mebd discovers that her husband has one more bull than she does.

Celtic chieftains spent quite a bit of their energy stealing cattle from one another. They even had a special word for this activity, *táin*. (Cattle raiding wasn't just an amusement for the ancient Irish; modern Irish people were stealing one another's cattle well into the twentieth century.) Anyone whose cattle got stolen had to try to retrieve them, which occasioned many heroic expeditions and battles.

# 10 } The Seat of Ancient Kings

Tara is a hill in County Meath that was the seat of ancient Irish kings. It was considered the center of Ireland. People buried their ancestors in mounds surrounding it and periodically gathered there for festivals and rituals. Kings and their armies would gather there before marching to war.

Tara was special because it was the home of the *Lia Fáil*, or "Stone of Destiny." It was used to identify rightful kings—it shrieked if the feet of the rightful king rested on it.

Ireland has tons of forts scattered all over the countryside, many of them built during the Bronze or Iron Ages and used for many centuries thereafter. The number and ingenuity of these forts suggest that the ancient Irish considered defense a high priority, though some experts think they were more likely built to impress. The most common form is the ring fort. These forts were built on top of circular mounds of earth with a wooden fence running around the circumference of the mound at the top and a moat surrounding the bottom.

Some forts were built entirely of stone or on the edges of cliffs, which provide a natural barrier to attack. Others, called crannogs, were built on artificial islands in the middle of lakes or bogs. They were used as late as the seventeenth century.

# 11 } Brehon Laws

The best picture we have today of ancient Irish social organization comes from the Brehon laws, which were written down in the seventh and eighth centuries C.E. These laws describe a very structured society, with several classes of people and clearly defined punishments for infractions.

For many years, historians believed that the Brehon laws came from the pre-Christian pagan past—possibly from the druids—and that they summarized centuries of laws and beliefs transmitted orally long before they were written. More recent scholars suggest that the Brehon laws were written by later Christians, who combined ancient Irish practice with foreign information and the Bible to create laws for the Irish people.

This would mean the Brehon laws as described might not have entirely reflected the reality of Celtic society, but instead the Irish society of some centuries later. Still, many of the principles would have applied to the Celts, especially the emphasis on social status, honor, and recompense for offenses.

# 12 } The Celtic Class System

There were five classes of Irish people. At the top were the nobles, who belonged to the dominant families and owned property. Below them were ordinary freemen, who rented the land and farmed it, and then base clients who had fewer rights; the lords would give their clients cattle, and in return receive rents and other services. At the bottom were slaves. The fifth class of people was the group of learned men, including doctors, judges, poets, and craftsmen. Members of this group enjoyed special privileges and could move most freely outside their own clans.

Brehon laws applied to civil, criminal, and military matters. They delineated five major classes of people and their rights and duties. All relationships, such as between landlords and tenants, parents and children, and masters and servants, were carefully regulated. Professionals were required to charge only the fees set by law, and they were ranked according to the status of their profession.

A person who injured another was required to compensate his victim for the loss or to have the person nursed back to health at his expense. Brehon law generally did not otherwise punish wrongdoers. People could kill outlaws who had committed serious crimes, but kings could ransom these outlaws and get them freed of obligation—if, for example, a king's ally had committed some atrocious crime and another noble wanted to kill him, the king could ransom the ally and get him off the hook.

## 13 } The Learned: Druids

The druids were an ancient caste of learned men. What they learned and what they did has long been a matter of much discussion and debate. Herodotus claimed that they were descended from Noah, originated in the western Danube region, and espoused Pythagorean philosophy. Pliny and Tacitus noted their fondness for the oak and their refusal to worship the gods under roofs. Julius Caesar described their schools, where they memorized vast amounts of information, and their sacrificial practices, which involved placing humans or animals in wicker cages and burning them alive.

The Romans distrusted the druids and did their best to put them down. In 61 C.E. the Roman Suetonius rounded up a number of druids and killed them, and that ended druidism in Roman territory (which didn't include Ireland). But the druids were too fascinating for people to forget them; many still think of the megalithic dolmens as druid altars, where the ancient priest-magicians sacrificed their victims.

In Irish legends, druids can predict the future by interpreting the actions of birds; they use this information to tell their leaders when to march into battle. They wear white robes and sport long beards.

One of the most famous is the druid Cathbad in the *Táin Bó Cuailnge*. In some versions of the story, he was the father of King Conchobar of Ulster (or Conor mac Nessa). Cathbad ran a school of druidry with eight students. After the hero Cuchulain accidentally killed his own son in battle, the soldiers of Ulster (on Cuchulain's side) feared he might kill them in his frenzied grief; Cathbad saved the army by casting a spell on Cuchulain to make him think the waves in the ocean were warriors, so he would fight them and expend his anger there.

## 14 } Celtic Art and Poetry

The Celts produced some spectacularly beautiful art. Much of their best work was done in metal. They applied the same attention to intricate detail to their poetry. Poets, like great craftsmen, were honored members of society, welcome in any noble home.

Celtic metalwork is intricately decorated. Celtic smiths worked in gold, iron, and bronze. The Celtic aristocrats liked to have nice things on hand to give as gifts to honored guests, which would bring great honor to the giver, and they especially liked finely wrought metal.

Celtic men and women wore heavy necklaces of twisted gold, called torques. These became status symbols, and the gods were also represented as wearing them. Celtic burial sites are full of decorative pins called fibulae, which are similar in design to the modern safety pin. Archaeologists have also discovered mirrors, combs, and a beautiful little model boat with oars. Many of these artifacts are elaborately decorated with the distinctive spirals and interweaving designs that the Celts are famous for.

Celtic smiths must have been very skilled to produce their works. They used the lost-wax casting technique—molding an object out of wax, surrounding it with clay, baking the whole thing so the clay hardened and the wax ran out, and then pouring in metal to form the object. They also formed objects out of sheets of metal, hammered thin and then cut and formed into the desired shape.

Celts held their craftsmen in high regard. Craftsmen belonged to a special privileged class of learned men, and the ordinary rules of serfdom and allegiance to a lord did not apply to them. They traveled from patron to patron plying their trade, and their status protected them from assault.

Poetry was extremely important to the ancient Irish. Poets, like craftsmen and judges, belonged to the privileged class of learned people. Poets preserved the history of the clan and of Ireland, including lore of the gods and the genealogy of the ruler. The ancient myths and legends were preserved by countless generations of poets, who memorized them and recited them to their listeners.

Poets came in several grades; a poet of the highest status was equal to any chieftain. Training to become a poet took years and involved memorizing thousands of lines of verse. Poets also had a reputation for knowing something about magic and prophecy. A patron would expect a poet to sing his praises, but he had to be careful; poets demanded large rewards, and an unsatisfied poet could create burning satire that could ruin a chieftain's reputation.

## 15 } Celtic to the End: The Never Conquered Nation

The Romans never saw a land they didn't want to conquer, but they never conquered Ireland. Julius Caesar initiated contact with Britain in 55 B.C.E., and for over a century the Romans planned to conquer the whole island. Though some Britons became Romanized, many locals didn't appreciate being colonized and fought their conquerors tooth and nail. The Romans couldn't keep enough troops on the island to hold them at bay. They had other frontiers to guard, after all. By 122 C.E., Hadrian had decided it would be wise to wall off Scotland to keep the barbarians separate from Romanized territory. Over the next two centuries, Rome gradually lost control over Britain.

The Romans knew Ireland existed; Ireland's Latin name is *Hibernia*, which might mean "Land of Winter." (Another theory holds that it comes from Iberia, or Spain.) Julius Caesar mentioned Ireland in his *Commentaries*, but just to note that it was less than half the size of Britain. The Greek geographer Strabo claimed that Ireland was on the edge of the habitable earth and that the inhabitants of the island were complete savages living a miserable existence due to the cold climate. The Roman Tacitus, writing around 100 C.E., thought Ireland was very much like Britain. In the late first century C.E., Agricola, a Roman governor of Britain, considered conquering Ireland and even did reconnaissance; he decided that the Romans could take the island with just one legion of soldiers, but it probably wouldn't be worth the effort.

But the Romans never tried to conquer Ireland. The distance from Rome was too great and the potential payoff too uncertain, and they already had their hands full with Britain. And so the Irish remained Celtic.

## 16 } The Celtic Pantheon

The Celts had many myths and legends. Celtic myths tell the stories of gods and goddesses and of ancient heroes—just like ancient Greek myths, but with a uniquely Celtic spin on things. These stories explain the origin of the Irish people, the relationship they had with their deities, and why certain people and places were more important than others.

Most of what modern people know about Celtic mythology didn't come straight from the Celts themselves, because they didn't write down any of their stories. Scholars over the past two millennia have cobbled together a picture of Celtic beliefs by combining archaeological evidence, details from Irish legends, and the writings of contemporary observers. Julius Caesar and other classical authors recorded a great deal of information on Celtic mythology, which is still useful today.

The Celts believed that there were many different gods and goddesses and that these deities had relationships with one another and with humans. There were gods of love, writing, light, death, and, of course, war.

## CELTIC GODS
The Celts had a number of gods; here are a few of them:

- **The Daghdha**, or "Good God," was the chief god of the Irish pantheon. He carried a club that could both kill and bring people back to life, and he had a giant magic cauldron that was always full of food.
- **Donn** was the god of the dead. The druids claimed that all people were descended from him.
- **Oenghus** was the son of the Daghdha. He was a handsome young man and functioned something like a god of love.
- **Oghma** invented the ogham alphabet, a system of writing used by druids.

- **Lug** was the sun god, god of genius and light. He was the hero Cuchulain's father. Julius Caesar thought that Lug was the most important Celtic god.
- **Nuadhu Airgedlámh** is an ancestor god-king. He lost an arm in battle and replaced it with one made of silver.
- **Dian Cécht** was the "Divine Physician." Mortally wounded people could be cast into a well, and he would sing over it, whereupon they would come out again healed.
- **Boibhniu** was the leader of three craftsman gods. He was also the host of the Otherworld Feast, where he served a drink that made people immortal.
- **Manannán** was a sea god. He oversaw the journey over the sea to the otherworld.

These were not the only Celtic gods. Many others existed, though not all their names have been recorded. There are still strange statues in Ireland that depict fearful beings, many with two or three faces; who they were or what they did, no one knows.

## Celtic Goddesses
The Celtic pantheon included a number of female deities. Many of them traveled in groups of three, such as the Macha-Mórrígan-Babd trio of war/fertility goddesses.

- **Anu, or Danu**, was the mother goddess and mother of the gods. She was connected with fertility and nurture.
- **Brigid** was the daughter of the Daghdha. She was goddess of fertility and patron of poets. She had two sisters, also named Brigid, who were associated with craftsmanship and healing; the three of them were often treated as one entity. Brigid's symbol was fire, and there was a fire kept alight for her in County Kildare from pre-Christian times until 1151. She later transformed into the Christian St. Bride, or St. Brigid.
- **A trio of sisters—Macha (MA-ha), Mórrígan, and Babd (bahv)—** were known as the Mórrígna. They were war and fertility goddesses; they played an important part in the war between the Tuatha Dé Danaan and the Fomorians.
- **Mórrígan** embodied war fury. There are a number of sites in Ireland that bear her name.
- **Babd** was both sinister and sexual; she sometimes appeared as a crow, sometimes as a hag, and sometimes as a beautiful young woman. She urged the hero Cuchulain to go fight his last battle that led to his death.
- **Scáthach** was the "Shadowy One." She taught the young Cuchulain all his magic.
- **Boann** was a water goddess who embodied the spirit of the Boyne River. She and the Daghdha had a child together—Oenghus, who functioned something like the god of love.

# 17§ The Otherworld

The world of Celtic gods and spirits was known as the otherworld, Mag Mell ("Plain of Honey"), Tír Tairngire ("Land of Promise"), and Tír na nÓg ("Land of Perpetual Youth"). It was a place of simple and sensuous pleasures. Everyone living there could eat as much as they wanted, and many heroes found loving women there. The cauldron of the Daghdha was there, and it was always full of food.

Heroes would occasionally make special trips to the otherworld; these voyages were called *imrama* (or *immrama*). A famous legend about an *imram* is the *Imram* Bran Maic Febail, the story of the Irish king Bran's journey to the otherworld (in other versions, the journey is to the Land of Women).

# 18§ Celtic Festivals

The Celts divided the year into two halves, the bright, warm half known as *samh*, or summer, and the dark, cold half called *gamh*, or winter. They punctuated the year with four festivals marking the different seasons:

- ☙ **Imbolc** (IM-bulk) took place on February 1. It was the feast of the goddess Brigid, associated with the birth of lambs and the lactation of ewes.

❧ **Beltane** (bal-thu-na) was celebrated on May 1. People lit bonfires, danced around maypoles, and made merry. This feast marked the start of summer.

❧ **Lughnasa** (LOO-na-sa) was a harvest festival held in late summer in honor of the god Lug. Festivities included games, drinking, dancing, matchmaking, and racing horses naked.

❧ **Samhain** (SOW-in) corresponds to modern Halloween and marked the end of summer. This is the day that tombs opened and ghosts walked about with gods and goddesses.

All four of these festivals correspond very closely to the solar equinoxes and solstices, all of which were easy to identify using the solar devices incorporated into various megalithic mounds. The Celts were masterful astronomers, given that they didn't have telescopes. They knew about the planets Mercury, Venus, Mars, Jupiter, and Saturn, and their year lasted 365 days.

# 19 ∫ Creation Myths

According to legend, the island of Ireland was invaded six different times in its prehistory. The story of these invasions is told in a body of myth called the Mythological Cycle (a title that came about in the nineteenth and twentieth centuries), much of which was recorded in the twelfth century in the

*Book of Invasions.* The ultimate consequence of all these invasions was a final battle between two groups of supernatural people, the Tuatha Dé Danaan and the Fomorians, and the establishment of civilization and social order.

The first invasion was led by one of the granddaughters of Noah (the biblical Noah who built the Ark), but her timing was bad; all of her people drowned in the great flood. Three hundred years later, another descendant of Noah, Parthalón, settled Ireland, building houses and clearing fields for farming. Parthalón's sworn enemies were the Fomorians, one-armed, one-legged monsters descended from Noah's cursed son, Ham.

Parthalón and his people all died of plague. Thirty years later, the third invasion arrived, led by a man named Nemhedh. They attacked the Fomorians, but most of them died in the effort. A few survivors fled to Greece, where they became slaves; they were called the Fir Bolg.

The Fir Bolg came back to Ireland, which they divided into the five provinces of the Celts. They established a kingship and ruled the land for thirty-seven years. Their last king, Eochaidh mac Eirc, was a perfect, just ruler; during his reign no rain fell, only dew; there was no year without a harvest; and nobody told any falsehoods.

## 20 ⟩ The Battles of Magh Tuiredh and the Invasions of Milesians

The Fir Bolg had a nice arrangement, but it was too good to last. Yet another group of people decided to invade Ireland: the Tuatha Dé Danaan.

The Tuatha Dé Danaan were the people of the mother goddess Anu. According to Irish legend, they arrived around 350 B.C.E. They came from four cities in ancient Greece, which is where they learned about prophecy and magic, the secrets of the druids. They brought with them four treasures:

- ⚜ **The cauldron of the Daghdha**—this vessel was always full of food.
- ⚜ **The spear of Lug**—this weapon ensured victory to its holder.
- ⚜ **The sword of Nuadhu Airgedlámh**—no enemy could escape from it once it was drawn from its sheath.
- ⚜ **The Lia Fáil**—known as the "Stone of Destiny," it shrieked when the feet of a lawful king rested on it; this ended up on Tara Hill, seat of Irish kings.

The Tuatha Dé Danaan were skilled in magic and fighting. Their leader, Nuadhu Airgedlámh, brought them into battle. But a Fir Bolg warrior named Sreng cut his arm off at the shoulder. Sreng made peace with the Tuatha Dé Danaan and agreed to leave them all of Ireland except for Connacht (or Connaught), where he led his own people.

Poor Nuadhu Airgedlámh couldn't be king anymore, because no one
with a physical defect (such as a missing arm) could be king. A man
named Bres got to be king instead. Bres was the son of the Fomorian king
Delbáeth; he had been adopted and raised by the Tuatha Dé Danaan,
and they obviously thought they could trust him. But there they were
mistaken.

Bres, the Fomorian, ruled the Tuatha Dé Danaan for seven years. This
was a lousy time for the Tuatha Dé Danaan. The Fomorians demanded
a tribute of cattle, and the gods were reduced to menial labor; even the
Daghdha himself was forced to dig ditches and build a fortress for Bres.

Meanwhile, the Tuatha Dé Danaan were planning their recovery.
Dian Cécht, the "Divine Physician," made a new arm for Nuadhu out of
silver, which would allow him to be king again. After a poet named Cair-
bre mac Étain (son of Étain) sang a verse mocking Bres, he gave up the
kingship and went off to gather an army of his Fomorians. Nuadhu was
reinstated as king; he and the Daghdha and Lug got together to decide
how to get back at the Fomorians. (Lug had recently appeared at the
court, and he had impressed everyone so much with his skill in all arts,
creative and warlike, that they let him be one of their leaders.)

The Daghdha went to see Mórrígan at the festival of Samhain. She
was standing astride the River Unius washing herself. They made love
standing over the water, which gave that spot the name "Bed of the Couple." She told the Daghdha that the Fomorians were coming to attack the
Tuatha Dé Danaan and that he should bring his soldiers to her. She killed

the son of the Fomorian king and gave two handfuls of the blood to the Tuatha Dé Danaan before they went into battle. She and her sisters Babd and Macha went to the Mound of the Hostages at Tara and made the sky rain blood down onto the battle.

Lug led the Tuatha Dé Danaan in the second battle of Magh Tuiredh. The Mórrígan entered the fray, cheering on the Tuatha Dé Danaan and pursuing any Fomorians who tried to run away. Blood ran freely over the white-skinned warriors and the River Unius was clogged with corpses. Lug and his armies finally defeated the Fomorians and drove them to the sea.

After the fighting was over, Lug spared Bres in return for some information about agricultural techniques. The Mórrígan finished off the story by declaring victory for the Tuatha Dé Danaan and predicting the end of the world.

The conquests of Ireland didn't stop with the Tuatha Dé Danaan. They were themselves invaded by the Milesians, the sons of Míl, also known as the Gaels.

Míl came from Galicia in northwest Spain. His full name was Miles Hispaniae (Latin for "soldier of Spain"). His wife was named Scota ("Irishwoman"). A druid named Caichér had predicted that Míl's descendants would rule Ireland, and they did.

Míl himself didn't go to Ireland, but his sons did. The Milesians arrived in Ireland sometime after the Tuatha Dé Danaan had established themselves, perhaps between 350 and 250 B.C.E. They landed in southwest Ireland during the Feast of Beltane and fought a huge battle with the Tuatha Dé Danaan. They proceeded to Tara and clinched their hold on the country.

After the battle, a poet named Amhairghin divided Ireland between the two parties. The Milesians got the part that was above ground, and the Tuatha Dé Danaan got the underground. The defeated Tuatha Dé Danaan retreated to the hills and mounds to become the fairy people.

# 21 } *The Táin*

The Táin Bó Cuailnge (toyn boe cooley), or the Cattle Raid of Cooley, is one of the most fabulous epic stories to come out of ancient Ireland. It is set around the first century B.C.E. The oldest manuscript that records it is the *Book of Leinster*, written in the twelfth century. The Táin is part of the body of stories known as the Ulster Cycle. The story concerns the conflict between Ulster and Connacht, and the question of whether men can accept a female ruler.

One night, Ailill (ahl-il), the king of Connacht, and his wife, Queen Medb (mayv), lay in bed arguing over which one of them was richer. Ailill suggested that Medb had improved her lot by marrying him and that it was proper for a man to rule the kingdom instead of her, but Medb insisted that she was as rich and tough as any king. They couldn't agree, so that very night they did an inventory. They laid out their garments and jewelry and lined up the livestock. And for every possession Ailill put up, Medb put up one just as good, except for one thing: a beautiful, white-horned bull.

This bull had been born to one of Medb's cows, but it had left her herd because it didn't want to belong to a woman. Medb was devastated, and she decided then and there that she would get a bull to equal the white-horned one. The only bull as good as this one was the brown bull of Cuailnge, the property of Daire mac Fiachna, king of Ulster.

Medb sent messengers to Ulster requesting the loan of the brown bull for one year. She offered generous terms: fifty yearling heifers, a large piece of land, a fabulous chariot, and her own "friendly thighs." Daire agreed readily, but that evening Medb's messengers boasted that if he had not accepted her terms, they would have taken the bull by force. After that, the deal was off.

Medb wasn't particularly perturbed by this; she had sort of expected this to happen and quickly assembled a vast army. It marched off to Ulster to capture the brown bull.

The Ulster army started marching to meet its attackers, but on the way the soldiers were all struck by strange, debilitating pains, the result of an old curse by the goddess Macha. So instead of encountering an army, Medb's warriors met a single hero: Cuchulain (koo-hool-n).

## 22 } The Heroic Deeds of Cuchulain

Cuchulain was the Celtic Achilles. He was seventeen years old, handsome, and utterly fearless. He had grown up as a foster son of King Conchobar (konn-r) of Ulster. Cuchulain's name means "Culann's hound." He got this name because when the hound of Culann the smith attacked him, he killed it with his bare hands. Culann was upset because his watchdog was dead, and Cuchulain offered to do the job himself until he found a replacement canine.

When Cuchulain met the army from Connacht, he killed 100 soldiers single handed. Next, he fought a series of Medb's warriors in single combat; Medb had persuaded soldiers to fight for her by bribing them with anything from land, to her own daughter in marriage, to her own thighs, which she had previously offered in exchange for the brown bull. Her warriors found these rewards enticing enough, but Cuchulain defeated all of them.

Turning back toward Ulster, Cuchulain discovered Medb's forces leading away the brown bull. He killed the leader, but the rest escaped with the bull, much to Cuchulain's distress. He took to his bed and slept for three days and nights, while the god Lug (who happened to be his father) healed his wounds.

While Cuchulain slept, the army of Ulster fought Medb's forces. The Ulster side was winning, but in the process lost 150 soldiers. When Cuchulain woke up and heard about this, he was furious and was transfigured by the warp-spasm, a battle-rage that turned him into the most fearsome sight anyone had ever seen. Possessed by this rage, he slaughtered hundreds of warriors, women, children, horses, and dogs. No man from Connacht escaped uninjured, but Cuchulain came away without a scratch on himself.

Cuchulain was a fearsome opponent, but Medb finally came up with a way to get the best of him. She forced him to fight his foster brother, Fer Diad, whom Cuchulain loved more than any other man. She persuaded Fer Diad to fight on her behalf by promising him her daughter as a wife. The men fought for three days without either one gaining an advantage, and each one sent assistance to the other at night. On the fourth day, though, Cuchulain killed Fer Diad with the *gae bolga*, a frightful weapon that would expand into twenty-four barbs within a wound, like an exploding shell. Then Cuchulain sang a lament over his fallen friend.

The Ulster forces pursued Medb's army all the way to the border of Connacht. There, Cuchulain met Medb face-to-face and chose to spare her because she was a woman. But the conflict wasn't over.

Medb had sent the brown bull straight to Connacht to keep it safe. As soon as it arrived, it bellowed three times. The white-horned bull heard it and came racing to defend his territory. All the warriors watched this mighty duel, which lasted into the night and ranged over the entire island of Ireland.

In the morning, the brown bull reappeared, carrying the dead white-horned bull on his horns. He galloped back to Ulster, scattering bits of his enemy's flesh as he went. When he arrived at the border of Cuailnge, his heart broke and he died. Medb and Ailill made peace with Cuchulain and the men of Ulster, and there was no fighting between them for the next seven years.

Truce or no, Medb spent the years of peace scheming to get revenge on Cuchulain. During the cattle-raid wars, he had killed a man named Cailidín, who had six children. Medb sent off Cailidín's children to study sorcery. When they returned, she got them to make Cuchulain think that all of Ulster was overrun by invading armies. Deceived, Cuchulain prepared to go to battle.

Conchobar feared some trickery and sent Cuchulain to the Valley of the Deaf, where he wouldn't be able to hear the fake battle cries. The children of Cailidín redoubled their efforts to convince Cuchulain that battle was nigh, and Babd, one of the girls (and also a goddess of war), went to the hero in the shape of his mistress and asked him to fight the men of Ireland. Cathbad the druid and Cuchulain's real mistress tried to tell him that he had been bewitched, but he went off to fight anyway.

## 23 } *Conchobar and Deirdre*

Conchobar, king of Ulster, was not a pleasant character, especially not with his wife Deirdre, whom he met back in the days before the big cattle raid. Before Deirdre was born, Cathbad the druid predicted that she would be very beautiful but would bring ruin on the kingdom of Ulster. Conchobar liked the sound of the beautiful part, so he hid her away, intending to marry her when she was grown.

Deirdre grew up alone, away from the court. One day she saw her foster mother skinning a calf in the snow and a black raven drinking its blood. She said that she would like a husband with hair as black as a raven, cheeks red as blood, and a body white as snow. As it happened, just such a man lived nearby: Naoise, son of Uisneach.

Deirdre and Naoise got together and ran away to Scotland. They lived at the Scottish court for a while, but the Scottish king began to want Deirdre for himself, so they returned to Ireland. There, Naoise was killed by Conchobar's ally Eoghan mac Durthacht, and Deirdre went to Conchobar's court.

She spent a year there, never smiling or lifting her head from her knee. One day Conchobar asked her what she hated most, and she replied "you and Eoghan." Conchobar wickedly then decided to give her to Eoghan. As she was riding in a chariot with both men, she leaped out of the chariot and smashed her head to pieces on a giant rock.

## 24 } Finn MacCool

Fionn mac Cumhaill, or Finn MacCool, was a great warrior and a major hero of ancient Ireland. His stories come from the Duanaire Finn (the "Lays of Finn"), part of the Fenian Cycle. Scholars have long debated whether Finn was a real historical figure from the third century C.E., but the current consensus is that he was completely mythical.

Finn was the son of Cumhaill, king of Leinster; he served the high king Conn, who reigned at Tara. Cumhaill was head of the Fianna, an elite band of warriors. Men seeking admission to this band had to pass a test of skill, such as fending off six men with spears, armed only with a shield and a stick. All members had to swear an oath of allegiance to the high king. If one of the Fianna was killed, the dead man's relatives were supposed to let the Fianna avenge him.

After Cumhaill refused an order to attend a meeting at Tara, Conn declared war on him. While he was getting ready to fight, Cumhaill met Muirne, the daughter of a druid, and got her pregnant. Her outraged father vowed that Cumhaill would die in battle.

Cumhaill told Muirne to run away and hide someplace where she could raise the baby in safety. Another druid had foretold that this child, Finn, would be a great leader of the Fianna, and Cumhaill wanted to make sure that this came to pass. Then he died, slain by the king's ally Goll mac Morna.

Muirne fled to a cave and gave birth to Finn, who grew up vowing revenge on Goll mac Morna and all his clan. Finn went to study with a druid named Fionn. Fionn was perpetually searching for the salmon of knowledge, a fish that would bring boundless knowledge to whoever ate it. One day, Finn caught the fish and went to cook it for Fionn. A blister rose up on its skin, and he pressed it down with his thumb. He then put his thumb in his mouth to soothe the burn, and he realized that he now knew everything. From then on, whenever Finn didn't know something, he would suck his thumb, and all would be revealed to him.

Finn became leader of the Fianna. The Fianna loved the woods and wild animals. They cooked their meals in ovens of the Fianna, small, circular holes lined with stones and surrounded by low stone walls. (You can still find these all over Ireland.) Finn had two hounds that were actually his own nephews. His wife was a deer-woman from the otherworld. She raised their son Ossian (USH-een) in the wilderness; he grew up to be the poet of the Fianna and was a famous bard. (The stories about Finn are sometimes called the Ossianic Cycle because Ossian supposedly composed them.)

Finn and the Fianna had many magical adventures. They encountered ghosts and witches but always escaped with their lives. They got magical weapons from a giant with three arms, one foot, and an eye in the middle of his forehead; he was a fabulous blacksmith who could make blades fiercer than any made by humans.

When Finn was an old man, he got engaged to a beautiful young woman named Gráinne. She didn't want to marry him, so she cast a spell on Diarmait, the handsomest of the Fianna. Diarmait and Gráinne ran away together and lived happily for a while.

One day, all the Fianna went to hunt the magic boar of Beann Ghulban. This boar had been Diarmait's foster brother, and there was a prophecy that it would cause his death. Sure enough, the boar gored Diarmait and ripped open his belly. The only way to save his life was for Finn to bring him a drink of water in his hands. Finn went and got the water, but then he remembered how Diarmait had stolen Gráinne away from him, and he let it trickle out through his fingers. Diarmait died, and the god Oenghus took his body away to Brú na Bóinne, where he was buried in Newgrange tomb.

These Celtic myths have been around for a long time. Christians of the medieval period read and wrote down stories about Celtic heroes, adding their own Christian twists. Irish storytellers have always loved these legends and embellished them, creating scenarios in which pagan heroes from ancient days encountered Christian saints from a later time. Irish patriots of a more modern day took mythical characters as models for heroism. All of these myths have helped the Irish create a sense of their own unique Irishness.

PART 2

# The Arrival of Christianity (and the British, Too!)

It's impossible to understand the spread of Christianity in Ireland without examining the lives of the men and women who made it their life's work to teach others about their new faith—the lives of the Irish saints. It is not known what actually happened and what was added by imaginative storytellers. But that's no reason to dismiss the stories of saints as pure fancy.

# 25 } Christianity Arrives

The Roman Empire formally accepted Christianity when the emperor Constantine converted in 312 C.E. (Although there had been Roman Christians during the previous three centuries, they were persecuted and Christian practices were illegal.) As Christianity spread gradually throughout the empire, it percolated up through Gaul and into Britain. It arrived in Ireland sometime in the early 400s.

Although everyone knows that St. Patrick brought Christianity to Ireland, it's possible that someone beat him to it. In 431—the first reliable date in Irish history, as recorded by Prosper of Aquitaine—a Christian missionary named Palladius was ordained by the pope to go to Ireland as the island's first bishop. But St. Patrick also supposedly arrived in Ireland as bishop around this time—432 is the traditional date for his arrival. So who was this Palladius person?

No one knows. There is nothing else written about Palladius. Patrick, on the other hand, left behind a written record of his accomplishments. The medieval Irish all credit St. Patrick with bringing Christianity to Ireland. Some people think Palladius and St. Patrick were the same man, or that Palladius's deeds have been subsumed into the St. Patrick legend. Some people even suggest that St. Patrick never existed.

# 26⟩ *Who Was St. Patrick?*

Irish tradition credits St. Patrick with bringing Christianity to the Irish and transforming the island from a wild warrior society to a peaceful, scholarly kingdom. Not much is known about his life, or whether he existed at all. Most of what modern scholars know about the historical Patrick comes from his "Confession", an autobiographical sketch he (supposedly) wrote toward the end of his life. It's very short, and actually pretty readable, though some parts of it are incomprehensible—Patrick wasn't very good at writing Latin. Patrick never mentions dates, so any dates that scholars claim for his deeds are just guesses.

Patrick's family was of British Celt (Briton) ancestry, and had lived in Britain for several centuries. His father was a well-to-do landowner, and Patrick probably grew up as a privileged young man, waited on by servants and educated in the classical tradition as it survived in Britain at the end of the Roman Empire. His family was Christian; his father was a deacon and his grandfather a priest. Young Patrick was not a pious youth. By his own account, he had turned his back on the Christian god, and he committed some serious, unknown crime in his midteens (more on that later).

When Patrick was almost sixteen, he was captured by a group of Irish slave traders and was sold into slavery in Ireland. Patrick spent the next six years herding sheep alone in the hills, hunger and cold his constant companions. In his desolation, he turned to God and prayed constantly.

One day God spoke to Patrick, telling him that his ship was ready to take him away from Ireland. It was not nearby, but in fact 200 miles away (which is unlikely, since very few places in Ireland are 200 miles from any body of water). Patrick set off on foot over the countryside, taking a great risk by running away from his master; he had no idea what he was headed for, but Patrick had no fear.

He reached the coast and found a ship ready to set sail. He asked the captain if he could sail with them, and the captain brusquely refused. So Patrick returned to the hut where he was staying and started to pray. Before he had finished his prayer, the sailors called him back and said that he could sail with them.

The ship sailed for three days and then landed. It's not clear where; Patrick reports that he and the sailors wandered "in a desert" for twenty-eight days, and there's no place three days' sail from Ireland that matches that description. Some scholars have suggested that they landed in Gaul (modern France) after it was ravaged by barbarians in 407; others think it more likely that they were making circles around Britain.

In any case, they had nothing to eat. The captain turned to Patrick and asked him what his Christian god could do for them. Patrick admonished him telling him, to put his faith in God and ask Him for food. Sure enough, a whole herd of pigs came running across their path. The sailors killed and cooked a few, and their problems were solved.

Eventually, Patrick got back to his parents, who were overjoyed to see him after so many years and begged him never to leave them again. But

Patrick discovered that home wasn't home anymore; he had changed too much in the last few years to feel comfortable resuming his life as a British landowner.

One night, he dreamed about a man named Victoricus, whom he had known in Ireland. Victoricus gave him a letter entitled "The Voice of the Irish." At the same time, Patrick heard the voices of Irish people calling him back to them. He knew that Ireland would be his destiny.

He left home again and studied for the priesthood. Some scholars think he went to Gaul, while others are sure he stayed in Britain, but it doesn't really matter. Patrick struggled with his coursework. His education had been interrupted by his abrupt enslavement back when he was a teenager, and he never did make up the ground he had lost; in his later writings, he often laments that his Latin is not very good and that he is uneducated. But he managed to learn the required material and was ordained a priest.

Now a priest, Patrick went back to Ireland as its bishop, one of the first Christian missionaries in history; the traditional date for this journey is 432. There was a lot for him to do in Ireland. The Irish were still barbarians, worshipping Celtic gods, raiding one another's cattle, and abducting slaves. Patrick was genuinely concerned about these problems; he found slavery to be particularly bad for women (his respect and concern for women made him very unusual among early medieval leaders).

Patrick was incredibly successful. He converted thousands of Irish to Christianity, established monasteries, and ordained priests all over the island. He placed bishops next to local kings, both to improve the

Church's position with the Irish and to have someone to keep an eye on the worst raiders and warriors. By the end of his life, the Irish had stopped their endless tribal warfare and the slave trade had ended.

Converting the Irish wasn't always easy. As the Romans left Britain, local British kings grabbed the abandoned territory and took over the piracy trade. One British king named Coroticus attacked in northern Ireland and killed or carried off thousands of recent converts. Patrick sent some priests to Coroticus to ask for the return of his people, but the king only laughed at them. Patrick responded with his "Letter to Coroticus," one of the two pieces of writing he left behind, in which he took the king to task for visiting this horror on his people. He also excommunicated him from the Christian faith, the worst punishment a priest could inflict on a believer. Patrick knew firsthand what it meant to be a slave, and his genuine love of his flock and grief at their suffering comes through in his prose quite clearly.

Over time, Patrick developed into a legendary figure. As the patron saint of Ireland and founder of Irish Christianity, he has been credited with numerous deeds. Here are a few of them:

- **He banished snakes from Ireland**—standing on top of Croagh Patrick, a hill in County Mayo, he rang a bell, and all the snakes in Ireland fled.
- **He used the Irish shamrock**, a three-leafed clover, to teach his converts about the Trinity, the one-in-three union of God, Jesus, and the Holy Spirit.

    ❧ **He argued with High King Laoghaire** at Tara and won for the side of Christianity.

    ❧ **He was on speaking terms with both God and an angel,** and once climbed Croagh Patrick to speak with God.

    ❧ **He wrote the lovely prayer** known as "Saint Patrick's Breastplate."

None of these myths can be verified, at least not as they are described today. The shamrock story appeared centuries after Patrick's death, and the "Breastplate" was probably written in the seventh or eighth century. It is possible that Patrick did face down a king over some issue of Christianity, but probably not as it is told in the famous story about Laoghaire.

# 27} St. Brigid the Generous

Brigid of Kildare was one of Patrick's converts to Christianity. She became abbess of a huge monastery that admitted both men and women. Some historians say she was actually a bishop. Most of what we know about St. Brigid is not historical fact, but it is fairly certain that Brigid was an immensely powerful woman who did a lot to advance Christianity in Ireland.

    Brigid's father was an Irish nobleman. She converted to Christianity while still living at home. The first thing she did was to start handing out her father's food and goods to beggars. Her father was furious; he tossed her into his chariot and drove off to see the king of Leinster, to offer him Brigid as a wife.

When they got to the king of Leinster's palace, Brigid's father went in alone to see him. Out of respect, he first took off his sword and left it in the chariot with Brigid. While her dad was in the castle negotiating her marriage, a leper came up to Brigid and asked her for help. The only thing available was her father's sword, so she gave him that.

Her father and the king of Leinster then came back out. Of course, her father immediately noticed that his sword was gone and wanted to know what Brigid had done with it. When he found out, he flew into a rage and beat her.

The king of Leinster, intrigued by this unusual young woman, stopped her father from hitting her and asked her why she gave away his things. She replied that if she could, she would steal all of the king's wealth and give it away to the poor. Not surprisingly, the king decided not to marry her after all.

Brigid's monastery was huge; it contained a school of art and a scriptorium that produced gorgeous religious manuscripts. Brigid never abandoned her desire to help the poor, and her monastery was famous for its hospitality. After her death it turned into a center of pilgrimage, almost as big as a city. It became a place of refuge for anyone in Ireland, where people fleeing invaders could find safety and where kings could store their treasures.

Brigid was radical in more ways than one. She admitted both men and women to her monastery, and she seems to have performed all the duties of a priest. This was an outrage for the Catholic Church, which has never approved of female leadership, though people broke many rules in far-flung Ireland in the early medieval days.

Brigid is sometimes called the Mary of the Gael. In one legend, she shaped a cross out of reeds to teach people about Christianity, much like St. Patrick used the shamrock to explain the Trinity; today, Irish people still keep St. Brigid's crosses. Brigid's feast day is celebrated on February 1.

February 1 is also the Celtic feast of Imbolc, dedicated to the Irish fertility goddess Brigid. Coincidence? Certainly not—the Irish incorporated many aspects of their pagan Celtic religion into their version of Christianity. Another pagan-Christian combo associated with Brigid was St. Brigid's fire, which was started in ancient times and burned into the Middle Ages.

## 28 } St. Columcille, Felonious Monk

Columcille, usually called Columba by non-Irish writers, converted thousands of Celts to Christianity and founded a plethora of monasteries. But he didn't do this simply out of love of God; he committed some serious sins and then threw himself into God's work as a form of atonement. Part of his penance was permanent exile from Ireland, which turned out to be the key to his impressive missionary accomplishments.

Columcille's real name was Crimthann, which means "fox" in Irish. He was the son of a nobleman of the Conaill clan, and was well educated in his youth. When he had finished his secular education, he went to study with Bishop Finian in Clonard, Gaul.

Finian owned a beautifully decorated Psalter, and Crimthann fell in love with it. He wanted to copy it, but Finian wouldn't let him. So Crimthann stole into the darkened church at night and copied it in secret. He had no candle, but the fingers of his left hand shone with lights to illuminate his work. Sadly for Crimthann, he got caught, and King Diarmait (or Dermot) made him give the copy back to Finian.

Crimthann became a monk and took the name Columcille ("Dove of the Church"). He made a pilgrimage to the grave of St. Martin of Tours, a legendary founder of monasteries. Inspired by Martin's work, he returned to Ireland and began founding monasteries right and left. By the time he was forty-one, he had founded forty-one monasteries.

But Columcille wasn't a good, peace-loving Christian. King Diarmait had one of Columcille's followers killed, and Columcille got angry; he persuaded all his warrior relatives to go fight the king. They defeated Diarmait, and Columcille took this opportunity to reclaim the Psalter he had copied from Finian years earlier. It was thereafter called the Cathach ("warrior").

But a monk is not supposed to go to war. Columcille was excommunicated and told that he must leave Ireland forever. Three thousand enemy soldiers had died in the conflict, and Columcille set himself a penance of converting 3,000 pagans to Christianity. With this daunting task ahead of him, Columcille enlisted twelve followers and sailed away to the island of Iona, off the coast of Scotland.

Columcille and his followers had embraced the White Martyrdom, the sacrifice of leaving behind the land they loved best and moving to an unknown territory, there to fast and do penance in a monastery they built. Soon, they found themselves unaccountably popular. People from all over Ireland, Scotland, and Britain heard about this new monastery with the famous abbot, and they came to visit. Many of them decided to become monks themselves.

Columcille decided that Iona could only hold 150 monks. When there got to be too many men on the island, he would send off groups of thirteen monks to found new monasteries elsewhere in Scotland. Would-be monks kept coming, so Columcille kept sending off new groups of monastery founders. By the time he died, more than sixty monastic communities had been founded by his men all over Scotland, and he had met his goal of 3,000 conversions many times over.

## 29 ⎰ St. Columbanus, Missionary to Europe

Columcille had spread Christianity through Scotland; Columbanus (or Columban) took it even further. He took his mission to Gaul, through Switzerland, and into northern Italy, converting barbarians everywhere he went.

Columbanus was born in Leinster around 540. As a young man, he traveled to Ulster to study and then entered a monastery in Bangor, County Down. He worked and prayed there for twenty-five years.

Around 590, Columbanus and twelve companions went to Gaul to found a monastery there. He was so successful that he actually founded three: Annegray, Fontaines, and the important Luxeuil. He worked with the uncivilized barbarians living in the forest, trying to convert them to Christianity.

This went against the practice of the local bishops, who preferred to stay in larger towns and cities and preach to their local believers. The bishops disapproved of Columbanus and summoned him, but he refused to go; instead, he sent them a letter in which he basically told them that they weren't doing their jobs. In Columbanus's opinion, a bishop ought to be out in the countryside trying to reach the pagans.

The bishops conspired with the evil queen Brunhild of Burgundy to have Columbanus deported. He and his followers went to Nantes to catch a ship back to Ireland, but it sank. Columbanus and four companions survived and headed for northern Italy. In the Alps, his German translator, Gall, got sick and refused to go on. Columbanus had a big fight with him, and then left him behind.

By 612, Columbanus and his companions were in Bobbio (in Lombardy, Italy). There they built the first-ever Irish-Italian monastery. Columbanus spent the rest of his years writing outrageous letters to his fellow churchmen. He is best known to us through his extraordinary correspondence, written in impeccable Latin and thoroughly grounded in Scripture. He never stopped criticizing his colleagues, and he seemed to have had no sense of humility or respect for rank. He even sent letters of scathing criticism to two popes. Columbanus died in Bobbio in 615.

## 30 } Wild and Crazy Irish Saints

You can't swing a cat in Ireland without hitting a saint. Most towns and professions have their own patron saints who take a special interest in their affairs. For example, St. Mac Dara is patron saint of fishermen in the Aran Islands. Other saints became famous by founding monasteries or teaching other saints. St. Enda from the Aran Islands taught many holy men, including St. Ciaran. Others became famous for their miraculous deeds, great wisdom, and courage, or their unbelievable love of discomfort.

### Kevin of Glendalough, the Tree-Hugger
Kevin was a member of the royal house of Leinster. He was born around 498. As a boy, he was taught by three holy men, and when he grew up, he moved to Glendalough, a spectacular site in a valley surrounded by sheer cliff faces and between two lakes.

Kevin is said to have taken up residence in a tree. He was very close to the animals—once a bird even laid an egg in his hand. He later moved into a tiny cave called St. Kevin's Bed. He spent his days either standing naked in one of the frigid lakes or hurling himself naked into a patch of nettles.

Kevin's fame spread, and he soon had a number of followers who persuaded him to let them build a monastic community on the shore of one of the lakes. They got him to move out of his cave into a little stone hut that they built for him.

## ST. DECLAN

Declan brought Christianity to southeast Ireland in the fifth century. It's said that he was adrift at sea, praying, when a stone floated by with his bell and vestments. He vowed that he would land wherever the rock landed and would there find his resurrection. He and his stone washed ashore at Ardmore, County Waterford, and there his stone still sits on the beach today. It would cure the rheumatism of any believer (except a sinner) who could manage to crawl under it, a feat that would be difficult for anyone afflicted with that ailment.

## ST. CIARAN

Ciaran (or Kieran) was born in Connacht in 512 and became famous for founding the great monastery of Clonmacnoise in County Clare. Clonmacnoise was exceedingly isolated—it was surrounded by bog and could only be reached by river or by walking along a ridge called the Pilgrim's Road. (Bogs notwithstanding, this is another beautiful site.) This monastery flourished for 600 years as an international center of learning. It produced many illuminated manuscripts, including the *Book of the Dun Cow*, the earliest known manuscript in the Irish language; it was named after Ciaran's cow, which might have supplied the hide that bound it.

### St. Brendan the Navigator

Brendan was a very popular saint in medieval Europe. According to legend, he set out with twelve disciples in search of the land promised to the saints. At Clonfert, County Galway, he founded a monastery around 512. His adventures along the way, which included an encounter with a crystal column on the ocean and a passage through a curdled sea, thrilled generations of people in Ireland and Europe.

## 31 } Irish Blend: Christian Traditions

The early Middle Ages in Europe are often called the Dark Ages. But in Ireland, this period was a Golden Age, at least for Christian monks. The Irish Christians lived a peaceful existence, devoted to scholarship and prayer. A group of Irish monasteries became a destination for scholars from all over the Continent; they produced a body of astonishingly beautiful works of art and preserved classical learning for posterity.

Ireland is a long way from Rome. As a result, the Irish developed a form of Christianity that didn't follow Rome's rules to the letter. The Irish were much more open to different beliefs and accepting of nonbelievers. They didn't set as much store in the infallible authority of the church fathers, and they were more willing to allow women a say in how things would be run.

Early Irish Christians built their religion on top of a pre-existing culture and set of religious beliefs. The Celtic gods and the druidic traditions were still present, and everywhere people looked they saw the prehistoric mounds that were supposedly inhabited by the old deities. People still celebrated the old festivals, but put a new Christian veneer on them.

For example, Samhain turned into All Hallows' Eve, better known as Halloween; All Hallows' Eve and All Saints' Day are still celebrated by the modern Catholic Church.

After St. Patrick introduced Christianity to Ireland, many new Christians in the fifth and sixth centuries wanted to show how dedicated they were to their new religion. Patrick had told them stories of early Christian martyrs, men and women who were thrown to lions or murdered for their faith in other glorious, horrible ways. But Ireland was now peaceful, and no one was persecuting Christians there. So how could an Irish person match that level of commitment? Ever resourceful, they found a solution: leaving society and its comforts to commune with God alone.

The Irish came up with an intriguing theory of the kinds of martyrdom available to them, now called the "threefold martyrdom":

- ❧ Red Martyrdom: Red because the martyr sheds blood for faith's sake—this is the conventional martyrdom by torture and death.
- ❧ Green Martyrdom: Leaving the comforts of home to live in some isolated spot in the wilderness, studying Scriptures and communing with God.
- ❧ White Martyrdom: Leaving Ireland to lead a monastic life in some foreign land, the most extreme form of sacrifice.

For most serious Irish Christians, the Green Martyrdom was the most likely plan of action. They had read stories about Egyptian and Middle-Eastern hermits who had lived alone in the wilderness, fasting and doing penance, and they decided to adopt this model for themselves. They gave up material pleasures; in return, they hoped for grace in the next life. But they didn't count on becoming the most popular phenomenon to hit Ireland in the early Middle Ages.

## 32 } Monasteries in Ireland

One of the most notable features of medieval Ireland was its absence of cities. The Irish lived in the countryside, farming little plots of land and grazing their cattle, and they never settled down in large groups. On the Continent, cities served as gathering places for educated people and as nuclei for cultural exchange; bishops had their headquarters in cities and spent their time preaching to their local, relatively wealthy, urban flocks. In Ireland, monasteries began to serve this purpose, with predictably different results.

The earliest Irish monks went off to live by themselves as solitary hermits. But they didn't stay alone for very long. Word got out about their wonderful isolation and asceticism, and people with their own aspirations toward monasticism would come and ask to become their students.

Before long, a solitary ascetic would become the head of a small community. These groups built themselves little enclosures containing huts for the monks, a church for believers to hear Mass, and often a library. Many monasteries also included a guesthouse, where visitors could stay to learn about Christianity and pray with the monks or nuns. The hospitality of Irish monasteries was famous; visitors were always welcome, and monks and abbots were always willing to baptize new believers.

Monasteries actually looked like small towns. Many of them contained a number of small buildings surrounded by a wall. The most distinctive type of architecture from this period was a kind of hut shaped a little like a beehive, constructed of stones held together without mortar. The skill involved in building one of these was extraordinary, because the technique required balancing all the rocks perfectly; the monks grew so good at this job that some of their beehive huts remain standing today.

Medieval monastics' primary purpose was to worship, and worship they did—several times a day! The following is an outline of the traditional monastic services, or "offices":

- Matins, sung before daybreak (in the middle of the night)
- Lauds, sung at sunrise
- Prime, sung at about 6 A.M.
- Terce, sung at 9 A.M.
- Sext, sung at noon
- Nones, sung at 3 P.M.
- Vespers, sung at sunset
- Compline, sung right after Vespers

Monks had to get up twice in the night to walk over to the chapel and sing their offices. They complained about it, but that was the point—monastic life was supposed to include some suffering. But there would have been some reward even for people dragged out of their beds at midnight in midwinter—their prayer services were often done musically. The monastic offices are the origin of the famous Gregorian chants, beautiful a capella musical arrangements of psalms and other pieces of Scripture.

Latin, the language of the former Roman Empire, became the language of the Christian church. All religious documents and correspondence, including the Bible, were written in Latin, and the Mass was performed in Latin. The Irish monks who entered the Church in the sixth century spoke the Irish language, but all of them had to learn Latin in order to write.

The Irish had to start from scratch in learning their new language. New Christians in other parts of Europe had been in contact with the Romans and their traditions and often knew the basics of Latin; French and Spanish are largely derived from it. But the Irish language is not closely related to Latin. The Irish needed a book that taught Latin starting with the absolute basics.

This was apparently the first time this problem had ever come up—there weren't any basic Latin grammars. So the Irish took on the task of producing one (generations of students of Latin have them to thank for their suffering). An obscure scholar named Asper took a grammar by the Latin grammarian Donatus and adapted it for the Irish market.

This grammar, called the *Ars Asporii*, used a question-and-answer format to convey Latin sentence structure and vocabulary, but with an Irish monastic twist. The author removed all pagan terms and substituted the language of monastic life. The book was a huge success (for a Latin textbook); it was established as a key authority by the seventh century.

## 33 } Schools and Universities

One of the most important functions of monasteries was as schools. Monastic schools were well attended (mostly by boys). Some of the students were treated as foster children by the monks, living in the care of another family until they were ready to return to their homes and adult responsibilities. Many noble warrior fathers seem to have thought that their sons would be safer in a monastery than at home. Students had to find and prepare food for the monks and help out with the business of running the monastery. But most of their time was spent studying and working.

By the sixth century, Irish schools had a firm curriculum. Students studied Latin grammar, biblical exegesis, and the ecclesiastical calendar. A monastery's library would contain several basic texts, including the Bible (the Latin Vulgate, translated by St. Jerome), various commentaries on Scripture, Jerome's book on early Church writers called *De viris illustribus*, and a church history by Eusebius. The computation of the ecclesiastical calendar was of special interest to Irish monks and medieval religious scholars in general, and big monasteries would stock several works on the subject. The seventh-century scholar Columbanus mentioned calendrical problems in several of his letters.

## 34⟩ The Pre-Xerox Age: A Life of Copying

In the days before photocopiers and scanners, the only way people could copy a book was the hard way—by hand. Every book at a monastery, from the Bible to the textbooks used in the schools, had to be hand-copied. This took up much of the monks' time. Monasteries lent books to one another for the purpose of copying; often the borrowing monastery would make two copies, one for itself and one for the lending monastery.

The early monks didn't write on paper, but on parchment, which is made of dried sheepskin. The most important texts sometimes got transcribed on vellum, which is made from dried calfskin.

The Irish monks, copying away in their monasteries, didn't realize that their work would have lasting implications for all of European history. But they did, in fact, preserve classical learning for posterity.

After the Roman Empire fell, the state of education fell along with it. The Romans and the Greeks were consummate scholars and wrote learned treatises on all manner of topics—history, science, and literature. In the early medieval period, much of that literature was in danger of being lost forever. People on the Continent didn't know its importance, and many of them were too busy fighting barbarians, or becoming barbarians themselves. In Ireland, though, peace prevailed.

The Irish monks even transcribed their own local epics in Irish. These texts, including Irish epics such as the Táin Bó Cuailnge, are some of the earliest examples of vernacular literature.

The Irish monks weren't content to simply copy texts. They had to embellish them, to make them into works of art. They were fascinated with the shapes of letters and experimented with ways of making them more beautiful. They invented a script called Irish miniscule that was easier to read and write than many other medieval scripts had been; it was so successful that monasteries across Europe adopted it.

Monks also used color and drawings to decorate their texts, in a technique called illumination. They took their inspiration from ancient Celtic art, the spirals and zigzags that decorated the tombs at Newgrange and myriad metal objects. Using paints made from various pigments, including insects, they applied brilliant colors to their complicated drawings to create books that would dazzle the eye of the reader. Letters themselves became fabulously embellished; sometimes an entire page would be filled with a fabulously decorated single letter. Sometimes artists even decorated their pages with gold leaf that would catch the light and literally "illuminate" the text.

Ireland is home to several famous illuminated books that survive today:

- The *Book of Kells*
- The *Book of Armagh*

✤ The *Book of Durrow*
✤ The *Book of Dimma*

Each of these is a masterpiece by the standards of any day, full of illustrations and text painstakingly planned and executed.

# 35 } The Book of Kells

The *Book of Kells* is probably the most famous illuminated manuscript in the world. Its several volumes contain the four gospels and supplemental texts. The reason for its fame is the extraordinary art that graces almost every one of its pages.

The history of the *Book of Kells* is murky and full of legend, but the most common story is that it was written around 800 at St. Columcille's monastery on Iona, off the coast of Scotland. Vikings started hitting the monastery at about this time, and the monks fled with the book to Kells in Ireland. The first written reference to the book is a report from the year 1007, noting that the great "Gospel of Columkille" had been stolen and found soon after, buried in the ground. At some point, the metal shrine containing the book disappeared, perhaps stolen by Vikings. Along the way, the book lost about thirty of its folios.

In 1661, the *Book of Kells* ended up at Trinity College in Dublin. It wasn't always cared for properly and was occasionally mistreated; in the eighteenth century, a bookbinder actually trimmed its pages, which caused irreparable damage. It was rebound in four volumes in 1953. Its modern keepers have been much more diligent about protecting it from light and moisture, and keep it in strictly controlled conditions. Astonishingly, given all the book has been through, it is still mostly intact, and the colors are still bright.

Today, the people of Kells want their book back. The librarians at Trinity College aren't sure that it would be cared for properly, but they have considered the possibility of returning the book to its medieval home. Meanwhile, it still resides in Dublin.

Medieval Ireland became known as the Island of Saints and Scholars. Irish monasteries such as Glendalough and Clonmacnoise were famous all over Europe, luring students from England and the Continent. Clonmacnoise was known as the University of the West. But it didn't last.

Beginning in 795, Viking raiders started coming to Ireland. They weren't interested in learning or art, but they knew where to find riches—in monasteries. Over the next 200 years, Vikings attacked and burned hundreds of monasteries and killed countless monks. Ireland's Golden Age was coming to an end.

Still, the Irish remember their medieval Christian forebears and their glorious heyday. They have carefully preserved the relics of that day, the exuberant decorated texts and works in metal. People travel from all over the world to visit Irish shrines and holy sites. And the world still has access to classical texts, which would not have been possible if Ireland had not created a group of joyful, imaginative scholars and an age of peace.

# 36} The Rise and Fall of Irish Dynasties

Early medieval Ireland was a site of battles, deadly rivalries, and relentless invaders. While monks led secluded lives in their monasteries, Irish lords were vying for rule of the island. When the Vikings arrived, some Irish lords fought against them, but others took the Vikings' side. It was in the midst of this complicated situation that the great hero Brian Boru emerged.

Ireland in its early days of Christianity was still ruled by the same Celtic noble families as before; the difference was that now they were Christian. Their new religion, however, didn't stop the old traditions of tribal warfare and cattle stealing. Irish historians used to claim that the tribal societies of pre-Viking Ireland had strict rules for warfare that limited the damage of conflicts, and that the Vikings ruined this state of relative peace. Historical evidence, though, indicates that the Irish were at least as violent and prone to ravage the countryside as their invaders.

The most powerful family during this period was the Eóghanacht, who had occupied the plain of Munster by the seventh century. Their home base was at the Rock of Cashel, in County Tipperary. "Cashel" is an Anglicized version of the Irish *caiseal*, which means fortress; it got this name because Cashel is a high hill covered with fortifications. (Cashel rivaled Tara as a seat of power during the medieval period.)

To the east of Munster lay Laigin, which became the modern province of Leinster. To the north lay the kingdom of Ulaid, which became Ulster. In the center was Meath, which was overtaken by members of the

Uí Néill clan, the ancestors of the modern O'Neills. To the west was Connacht, named after a relative of the Uí Néills named Conn Cétchatchach; this province was dominated by the Uí Briúin clan. The Uí Néills were particularly prolific; they eventually laid claim to all of Ireland and called their king the "high king."

Irish genealogy was anything but simple and clear. Kings took several wives and had many sons, thereby splitting royal families into several branches. These branches fought with one another and with outside enemies. Families rose and fell in power and there was no clear sense of national unity, whatever the Uí Néills might try to claim; there was no "Ireland" as such, only small kingdoms fighting and stealing one another's cattle.

## 37} Anglo-Saxons in Britain

After the Celts spread across central and western Europe, another group of people came in their wake. These were the Germanic people, who spoke a completely different language. They spread into the Baltic region, through northern Germany, Denmark, the Netherlands, and north into Norway and Sweden.

The people who lived in the southern part of that area spoke the Germanic languages, which eventually evolved into modern German dialects; the ones who lived in Scandinavia spoke Norse tongues, ancestors of modern Norwegian, Danish, and Swedish.

Around the time the Romans left Britain, the Germanic peoples started to cast longing gazes at the fertile island to their west. In 449 C.E., a whole passel of them got into their boats and sailed across the North Sea to Britain. Old English chronicles name them as the Angles, Saxons, and Jutes. They were fearsome people, eager for violence, and the native Britons (who were Celts) fled before their swords and fires. As they established themselves, people in Britain began to refer to them collectively as the Angles, or the English; this time in British history is known as the Anglo-Saxon period.

The Celts retreated to Wales, Cornwall, and Scotland, which, along with Ireland, are the few places that Celtic languages are left today. The invaders took over everything else, the most fertile parts of Britain. The extent to which they overwhelmed the natives is evident in the scarcity of Celtic words in the English language.

## 38 ⸘ Bring On the Vikings

Once the Anglo-Saxons had settled in England, they calmed down somewhat. They built towns, converted to Christianity, stopped raiding, and behaved like "civilized" people. But in the eighth century, they were attacked by another group of invaders: the Vikings.

The Vikings were Scandinavian people from Norway, Sweden, and Denmark, basically a northern version of the earlier Germanic invaders.

Between 750 and 1050, Scandinavians spread all over northern Europe and into the Atlantic, establishing colonies in faraway Iceland, Greenland, and even Labrador. They were collectively called Vikings, which either comes from the Norse word *vik*, meaning "bay," or the Old English word *wic*, meaning "camp." Either is possible: Viking boats were often found in bays, and they set up camps across Western Europe.

The Vikings called themselves Ostmen, or "men from the east." They were excellent sailors, and they had a reputation for raiding, stealing, and burning whatever they found in their way.

The Vikings first hit Ireland in 795, landing their technologically advanced warships at Lambay Island near the site of modern Dublin. From there they launched attacks up and down the coast, first concentrating their raids on the northern and western seaboards. Between 820 and 840, they ventured down rivers into the interior of the island, attacking churches for booty and captives.

The Vikings developed a quick and efficient style of hit-and-run attack. Although the Irish fought back, the Vikings were at least as ferocious as the Celts and much better armed. Also, the Irish were never unified against the Vikings; the wealth of the monasteries attracted the attention of several Irish lords, and sometimes monks found themselves under attack by their own countrymen.

The monks responded by fortifying their monasteries, reinforcing wooden walls with stone and adding other defensive structures. The most famous of these fortifications were round towers, tapering stone cylinders

100 feet high that doubled as bell towers and watchtowers; a five-story staircase led up to the top.

The entrances to these towers were raised off the ground and could only be entered by climbing a ladder. When the monks were under attack, they could all climb into the tower and then pull up the ladder after themselves. Then they could climb up to the top and watch their monastery burn as they themselves slowly starved; the hope was always that the invaders would leave before that happened.

## 39 } Dublin Is Founded

Eventually the Vikings stopped raiding and started settling down. They built settlements called *longphorts*, which were similar to naval camps. They used these encampments as bases for further attacks, but also as foundations for towns. The Vikings founded Dublin around 840, when they spent the winter moored there. The city's name comes from the words "Dubh Linn," which means "Black Pool." Dublin became the Vikings' chief base in Ireland, the place from which they launched raids on unconquered lands.

One of the things that prevented the Irish natives from defending themselves against the Vikings' earliest onslaughts was the endless state of mild to severe warfare that they maintained against one another. They couldn't stop arguing among themselves long enough to join forces against their common invaders, nor did they have any sense of a single Irish nation.

As the Vikings became more settled, though, they became more vulnerable to attack; people without property have nothing to defend, but someone with a house and farm has to keep watch over them. Norse Vikings and Danish Vikings fought over the same Irish territory. Starting in about 850, Irish kings began to launch their own raids on the Vikings with some success. A funny thing happened around that time; Irish kings and Vikings started to form alliances to fight other Irish kings, who had their own Viking allies.

By 900, the Vikings' Irish administration (such as it was) was in complete disarray, and the invaders had turned their attention to new raids in Iceland and northern Britain. This gave the Irish a window of opportunity, and they expelled the Vikings from Dublin in 902. Many Vikings left Ireland and bothered Britain instead for a few years.

Unfortunately, it was only a brief respite for the Irish. The Vikings came back in 914, took back Dublin, Munster, and Leinster, and spent another twenty years in power. After 950 they ceased to be much of a military threat, but they stayed on in the parts of Ireland that had become their home.

Despite the constant warfare, the reality is that most Irish people lived most of their lives just as they had before the Vikings arrived. In fact, some people lived better; the Vikings brought with them a number of valuable ideas from the mainland. They built the first Irish towns, they brought fancy boat-building techniques, and they could coin money.

They used these things to help increase trade to and from Ireland, which brought in artistic influences from the outside.

When the Vikings returned to Ireland in 914, they built a new stronghold at Dublin two miles closer to the sea than their earlier settlement; apparently, they wanted to be able to escape more quickly if necessary. They planned the city carefully, laying out streets and houses with great attention to detail. There was even a rudimentary drainage system, which suggests the presence of a strong leader in charge of urban development. By the late tenth century, the Kingdom of Dublin was one of the most important political units in western Europe.

## 40 } Life with Vikings

Thousands of people lived in Viking Dublin. There were merchants and craftsmen of all types—carpenters, shipwrights, blacksmiths, weavers, leather-workers, and others. Dublin's location put it right on the trade routes from Scandinavia down to England, and the Vikings traded vigorously with the people of England and continental Europe. They got wine, silver, and wool from England and Europe, which they sent on up to Scandinavia; from Scandinavia they received amber, ivory, furs, and slaves, which they moved on to European markets.

The Vikings also traded with the Irish people. This brought them into close contact with their new neighbors, and it appears that the two groups coexisted in relative harmony. (Some of those slaves traded by the Vikings did happen to be Irish, but the sad fates of a few individuals didn't necessarily hurt Viking–Irish relations on the whole; the Irish didn't all love one another.) The Irish taught the Vikings about Christianity. Members of the two groups married one another and sent their children to be fostered in one another's homes. Scandinavian artistic styles appear in Irish art around this time, and some of Ireland's most "characteristic" metalwork patterns of interlaced spirals with free-flowing tendrils, sometimes incorporating the shapes of animals, date from this period.

The Vikings displaced some of the Irish chiefs who had held sway throughout the island. This allowed other Irish families to try to take their places. The most important of these families were the rulers of Dál Cais in the lower Shannon region, who took over the lands of the displaced Eóghanacht.

In the first half of the eighth century, the Irish lord Cennétig, son of Lorcán, became king of north Munster, a region called Thomond; he died in 951. Cennétig had two sons, Mathgamain and Brian. Mathgamain added east Munster to his kingdom, along with the Viking-controlled areas of Limerick and Waterford. He became known as king of Cashel.

Mathgamain died in 976. His brother Brian succeeded him and became known as Brian Boru, the greatest of Ireland's high kings.

# 41 } What Would Brian Boru Do?

Brian was born around 941. His nickname, Boru, came from the old Irish word *bóruma*, which might have meant "of the cattle tribute." Or it might have come from the name of a fort in County Clare called Beal Boru.

Brian Boru was an excellent soldier. In 978 he led his warriors to victory in the Battle of Belach Lechta, in which the Dál Cais took the kingship of all of Munster from the Eóghanacht.

The rulers of other provinces took note of this; if Brian had all of Munster, he might want more territory. The high king of the Uí Néills, Máel Sechnaill, brought an army down to Munster and cut down the tree of Magh Adhair, a sacred tree on the Dál Cais family's royal inauguration site. This was a way of saying that the Uí Néills didn't recognize Brian's claim to the throne.

However, Brian refused to back down and quickly took over most of the southern half of Ireland. In 997, Brian met with Máel Sechnaill and the two kings agreed formally to divide Ireland between themselves. Brian got the south and the Uí Néills got the north.

But Brian wasn't content to stop there. In 1001, he defeated Máel Sechnaill and went about northern Ireland reinforcing his claim to it. In 1005, he went to Armagh and stayed at Emain Macha, the ancient capital of Ulster.

The problem with building an empire is that you can't watch your old territories while you're off conquering new ones. As Brian marched around, adding Ulster and other lands to his kingdom, Dublin and Leinster rebelled. He pushed them back in late 1013 and then fought a huge battle at Clontarf on April 23, 1014.

Soldiers came from the Isle of Man and other islands in the channel to help the rebel forces. Brian's army from Munster finally won, but Brian himself was killed. His followers took his body to Armagh, where they held a wake that lasted twelve days, and then buried him.

# 42 } An Ireland Unified

Many legends sprang up about the Battle of Clontarf. Later observers claimed that it was a battle between Irish and Viking invaders, with the king of the Irish winning a great victory for his nation and sacrificing his life in the process.

According to a popular version of the story written long after the event, Brian was too old to go to battle. While his soldiers fought, he knelt in his tent, praying with his Psalter. The Viking warrior Brodir ran into Brian's tent and hacked at the old king. An Irish boy named Tadhg raised up his arm to protect Brian, but the Viking sliced through his arm and cut off Brian's head in the same stroke. The boy's wound healed instantly when Brian's blood touched it. This episode portrays the Vikings as monsters and glorifies Brian's heroic, patriotic sacrifice as leader of the Irish resistance.

Modern scholars think it more likely that the battle was an internal conflict; Vikings no doubt were involved, but simply as soldiers for one side or the other. Brian himself was married to a Viking woman and might have given his daughter to a Viking in marriage. The men of Leinster were allied with the Vikings of Dublin. Certainly, the Vikings didn't leave Ireland after the conflict; they were too thoroughly integrated into Irish society by that point. Most historians now say that the Battle of Clontarf, though it made for some lovely literary interpretations, actually wasn't very important and held no real political significance.

Brian's own family was severely disadvantaged after the battle, mainly because most of them had died in it. His descendants, the O'Briens, managed to hang on to some power in Munster, but they were definitely not in a position to claim the high kingship.

Brian turned into a national hero. Later, Irish Nationalists would hold him up as an example of an Irish leader defeating foreign forces. They saw the period between Brian's death and the Norman invasion under Strongbow in 1170 as an age when there were no foreigners in Ireland.

Brian's victory did have some real repercussions for Ireland. The Uí Néills had lost their stranglehold on the high kingship, and though they recovered it occasionally over the next 150 years, the title itself had lost most of its meaning. Without the Uí Néills in power, the leadership of

Ireland was an open question, and many men were ready to take the job for themselves.

Economic changes in this period actually made warfare more dangerous. People were growing more food and producing more resources than they had in earlier centuries, and consequently the population was increasing. Lords required their growing populations to pay dues of livestock and money, a situation similar to the feudal system in effect in England and Scotland. With the added resources and manpower, chiefs had the wherewithal to march farther afield and sustain longer campaigns, with accompanying higher fatalities.

To defend themselves, Irish lords built larger castles and fortifications. The kings of the provinces struggled against one another, but no one came out on top. Every time it looked as if one man would prevail, one of his so-called allies would do something treacherous and it would all come tumbling down.

By 1170, however, the question of an Irish high king was irrelevant; the Anglo-Normans had arrived, and from that point on Ireland's destiny was inextricably linked with that of the larger island to the east—England.

## 43 } The Normans Are Here!

Just as the Irish were beginning to see the emergence of truly powerful high kings, something happened that altered the course of their history forever—the Normans arrived. The Norman English, who had recently consolidated their rule over Britain, began a conquest that eventually led to English domination of Ireland.

The ironic thing about the Norman arrival is that an Irishman invited them in. Dermot MacMurrough, king of Leinster, was unseated from power in 1166 by Rory O'Connor, king of Connacht. MacMurrough had heard that the Norman (derived from the term "North man," descendants of earlier Vikings) knights over in England were particularly tough, so he asked his English neighbor King Henry II if he could borrow some of them to get his throne back. Henry, alert to the possibilities of the situation, sent over Richard FitzGilbert de Clare—known to the world as Strongbow.

MacMurrough had guessed right about one thing—the Norman knights were tough. In 1170 Strongbow and his team of heavily armored knights plowed through the relatively lightly armed forces of Irish lords. The Irish probably could have put up a good fight if they'd joined together. But Ireland at that time was divided up among 100 or more kings, who tended to wait in their home territories for the Normans to arrive. When they did, the result was invariably Norman victory.

What MacMurrough didn't expect, though, was that the Normans might like Ireland and want to stick around. MacMurrough allowed Strongbow to marry his daughter Aoife, and when MacMurrough died in 1171, Strongbow had himself declared lord of Leinster. No one in Ireland could afford to object.

But someone back in England wasn't so happy about all this—the English king. Henry II watched Strongbow's string of successes and began to worry that his knight was getting too many ideas about his own power. So Henry sailed to Ireland to oversee the campaign and assert his own rights.

To consolidate the Norman victories, Henry declared Strongbow the king of Leinster but granted the province of Meath to Hugh de Lacy, a loyal knight. In 1175 Henry signed the Treaty of Windsor with Rory O'Connor, MacMurrough's old rival. The treaty declared O'Connor high king of Ireland, but it also said that he was a vassal of the king of England. Through these maneuvers, Henry established a system of competing lords in Ireland, who all ultimately owed their allegiance to the English Crown.

Over the next seventy years, Anglo-Norman knights extended English control over about three-fourths of Ireland. It wasn't so much an organized campaign as a series of advances by Norman adventurers who wanted their own fiefdoms. They only took property that they judged worth fighting for, so substantial portions of northwest Ulster and southwest Munster remained Irish.

The Irish probably thought they'd be able to take back their lands as soon as the Normans let down their guard, but the Normans did something the locals didn't expect—they built castles. Irish nobles generally moved around with their cattle, so they rarely built substantial structures. But Normans immediately set their serfs to building motte castles— earthen mounds defended by ditches and wooden towers. The mounds from these motte castles still dot the Irish countryside. Once these were in place, they built more substantial castles out of stone.

## 44⸗ The Irish Strike Back

Norman power in Ireland reached its peak around 1250 to 1275. After this, Irish lords began to reclaim their rights to the land. There were a number of reasons for this.

First, the definitions of Norman and Irish became vague. As Norman families spent a few generations in Ireland, they had less and less in common with their cousins in England. Distinctions of loyalty and family allegiance became blurred as the descendants of Norman settlers began to think of themselves as Irish.

Another reason was the impact of foreign politics. England was constantly fighting with Scotland and mainland Europe, and the king demanded that the Norman-Irish lords contribute men and money. This weakened the power of the Norman-Irish lords.

In one instance, the English war with Scotland led to a direct attack by Scots on Normans in Ireland, when the Scot Edward Bruce invaded Ireland between 1315 and 1317. While he didn't achieve any lasting conquests, his army inflicted such damage that many Norman towns did not recover for decades. His invasion also revealed to the Gaelic lords that the Normans were not unified.

The Irish kings took advantage of this Norman weakness. Starting from their strongholds in Connacht and Munster, they pushed Norman lords off their estates one by one. To improve the strength and discipline of their armies, the Irish lords hired tough mercenaries from Scotland called "gallowglasses." By the late fourteenth century, the Irish had regained much of their land.

The English king Richard II wasn't too happy about this. He personally led two reconquest expeditions in 1394 to 1395 and 1399, and he took back much of his lost territory. But the rebellion of Henry Bolingbroke (recounted in Shakespeare's *Richard II*) forced Richard to return home to England, where he eventually lost his throne and his life. With the English leadership gone, the Irish grabbed their property right back again.

For the next few decades, the English monarchs were too tied up in the War of the Roses to worry about Ireland, so the Irish lords continued to extend their power. By the early 1500s the area under English control had shrunk down to the city of Dublin and a small area surrounding it. This area of English influence was known as "the Pale."

## 45} I'm Henry VIII, I Am: Tudor Colonization

When Henry VIII became king of England in 1509, he also inherited the title "Lord of Ireland." English kings had carried this title for years without it meaning much. But, as people throughout Europe were to learn, Henry VIII was the kind of guy who liked to get his way.

The Norman-Irish lords had essentially been ruling themselves as independent monarchs for years. The most significant of these lords were the earl of Kildare and the earl of Desmond, both from the FitzGerald family (called the "Geraldine earls"), and the earl of Ormond from the Butler family. Garrett Og FitzGerald, earl of Kildare, served as lord deputy of Ireland for many years and was effectively the most powerful man on the island.

Henry VIII had three problems with Garrett Og: he was too powerful; his father had supported the York family's claim to the English throne over the Tudors; and he wasn't taking Henry's side in his fight with the Pope on whether he could divorce Anne Boleyn. So Henry had Garrett Og thrown into the Tower of London.

"Silken" Thomas Lord Offaly, Garrett Og FitzGerald's son, started a largely symbolic rebellion in 1534 to show that Henry needed the support of the FitzGeralds to govern Ireland. Henry took the symbolism literally and sent over an army to set them in line. Thomas's supporters backed off, and soon the FitzGeralds surrendered on the condition that they receive mercy. Henry agreed, and then promptly had most of them killed. The loss of Ireland's most powerful family left a power gap that Henry promptly filled with his own supporters.

## 46 } The Protestant Reformation

Religion added a new twist to the conflict in 1536, when the English Parliament passed the Act of Supremacy. This made Henry the head of the

Church of England and introduced the Protestant Reformation to the British Isles. England had been a Catholic country, but now it became officially Protestant. The Church of England was not especially different theologically from the Catholic Church, but it was different enough to provoke fights. Most important, Henry now refused to acknowledge the pope in Rome as the supreme leader on Earth; instead, Henry was now the head of his own church.

The Irish were still Catholic and wanted to stay that way. Although an Irish Parliament officially recognized Henry as the head of their church in 1537, most Irish maintained allegiance to the pope—and considered this ample reason to take up arms. This was the start of religious violence that has plagued Ireland for nearly 500 years.

## 47} Elizabeth I's Reign

This religious dispute became much more serious during the reign of Queen Elizabeth I. Elizabeth was an avowed Protestant. She spent much of her reign fighting with Catholic leaders in Rome and in Spain, who were constantly trying to topple her from the English throne. Under these conditions, she couldn't allow Catholics to attack her from her own back yard, so she gave tacit approval for Protestant adventurers to go claim land in Ireland from Catholic landowners.

The Irish were still resisting Protestant rule. In 1579, James Fitz Maurice Fitzgerald, cousin to the earl of Desmond, went to the Continent and brought back a small army to oppose Protestant rule in Ireland. Elizabeth responded by sending over a bigger army of English soldiers, who broke up the Irish rebellion. She confiscated the earl of Desmond's lands, had most of his family put to death, and resettled his old estates with loyal English subjects.

Elizabeth's greatest Irish challenge came with the revolt of Hugh O'Neill, earl of Tyrone. The O'Neills were an old Irish family originally from Ulster that once had claims to the high kingship of Ireland. O'Neill appealed for help in his rebellion to the king of Spain, who sent more than 4,000 soldiers to help fight England. Spain was Elizabeth's greatest enemy, so she raised a massive army of 20,000 soldiers to crush the rebellion. In 1601 her army defeated the Hiberno-Spanish force at Kinsale.

O'Neill and his fellow Catholic earls tried to mount another attack, but they couldn't gather sufficient forces to have any chance of victory. In 1607 they fled Ireland in the "Flight of the Earls."

James I became king of England, Scotland, and Ireland in 1603. He knew that O'Neill's strongest supporters had come from the north; Ulster at this time was the most Catholic and least Anglicized area of the island.

James I, therefore, decided to fix Ulster by settling it with loyal Protestants from England and Scotland, a plan that came to be known as the Ulster Plantation. The Protestant population that he settled there developed on very different lines from the Catholic Irish in the south. This led to considerable difficulties during the Irish struggle for independence, and more recently, during the Troubles in Northern Ireland.

## 48 } The 1641 Rebellion and Oliver Cromwell

The Rebellion of 1641 began as a political rebellion led by the prominent O'Neill family of Ulster, who wanted to recover its property from Protestants and overthrow the Puritan government then holding Ireland. The O'Neills had ordered their followers not to hurt anyone, but there was no stopping the crowd once it was unleashed. What started out as a political protest turned into an all-out attack on Protestant farmers as the Catholic commoners let their resentment bubble over. That November, Irish Catholics killed thousands of Protestants. No one knows how many died; estimates range from 2,000 (as suggested by some historians) to 150,000 (as claimed by Protestant pamphleteers). Many more lost their homes and property.

The attacks on Protestants by Catholics were bad, but they were nothing compared to the way they were described by English propagandists in London. They called it a "massacre." Pamphleteers inflated the Protestant death toll to nearly 150,000, and used extreme creativity in describing the horrors that the Catholics had inflicted upon them. The English public had always suspected that the Irish were barbaric, and this confirmed their suspicions. Now they were out for blood.

The 1641 rebellion coincided with a crisis in the English Parliament that eventually turned to civil war. King Charles I was beheaded, and the leader who emerged from the crisis was one of the most puritanical Protestants in England—Oliver Cromwell. Cromwell had no problem believing that the Irish Catholics had committed any number of atrocities, so he put together one of the most lethal armies in Europe to punish them.

The Irish leadership at this time was split between the Old Irish—led by Owen Roe O'Neill, Hugh O'Neill's nephew—and the Old English, led by the earl of Ormond from the Butler family. Although O'Neill and Ormond agreed that Ireland should remain Catholic, they opposed Cromwell for different reasons. Whereas O'Neill wanted Ireland to be independent, Ormond opposed Cromwell because he saw him as a usurper against the real king, Charles II. This ideological difference made it difficult for them to work together and ultimately aided Cromwell's campaign of conquest.

It took Cromwell until 1649 to clear up things at home sufficiently to launch his Irish campaign, but, when he came, he meant business. Cromwell's army of 20,000 was efficient, well armed, and prepared for a bloody war. The army's initial engagements were marked by extreme savagery; Cromwell wanted revenge for the supposed Catholic butchery of 1641, and he wanted to terrify the rest of Ireland into surrendering.

Here were some of Cromwell's less admirable achievements:

- He destroyed Drogheda, massacred the population, sent the heads of the leaders to Dublin on poles, and sold the survivors to slave plantations in Barbados.

- ❧ Also in Drogheda, he burned down St. Peter's Church to abolish the people who sought asylum inside; he later called his acts "a righteous judgment of God upon these barbarous wretches."
- ❧ Again at Drogheda, he had his soldiers kill the garrison commander by beating out the man's brains with the commander's own wooden leg.
- ❧ He massacred the people of Wexford, including 300 women seeking clemency at the town cross.
- ❧ He had all the Catholic citizens of Cork expelled from their homes.
- ❧ At Bishop's Rock in Inishbofin, off the coast of Connemara, he tied a priest to a rock and forced his comrades to watch as the tide washed over him.

Cromwell aimed to terrify the population, and he certainly succeeded. By 1653 the Irish resistance was completely destroyed.

One of Cromwell's goals in Ireland was to break the power of the Catholic Church, and for a time he succeeded. While on campaign, he had Catholic priests hunted down and banished. Throughout the country he had churches desecrated and their sacred books and art destroyed. The priests who escaped his army had to disguise themselves in order to remain on the island. Although Irish Catholicism was by no means destroyed, it would take decades to recover.

Once English control was firmly established in 1653, Parliament passed an act to confiscate all Catholic-owned land in Ireland. Cromwell wanted to transplant all Catholics to the western province of Connacht so that he could settle his own soldiers and Protestant supporters on the more fertile land of Munster, Leinster, and Ulster. Although the eventual settlement didn't force all Catholics off their land, thousands of families were forced to leave their homes and resettle on the rocky terrain of Connacht.

Cromwell lingers on in Irish memory. Up until modern times, Irish mothers would use Cromwell as a bogeyman to frighten their children—"eat your greens or Cromwell will get you!" He is also used to explain the sorry state of ruined buildings all across Ireland—"that used to be a beautiful castle, but then Cromwell showed up. . . ."

The radical Protestant initiatives of Cromwell's Parliament took a back seat after Cromwell's death. His son, Henry Cromwell, carried the banner for a while, but the English were getting tired of the Cromwells and their Puritanism. In 1660 came the Restoration, in which Charles II reclaimed the throne.

Charles II was more lenient toward the Irish than Cromwell had been. He restored some former supporters to their previous positions—notably the earl of Ormond, who had joined him in exile. He was a Protestant, however, and while he didn't share Cromwell's enthusiasm for radical social engineering, he wasn't interested in restoring land or position to Ireland's Catholics.

A wave of excitement went through Ireland when James II rose to the English throne in 1685. James II was the first Catholic monarch in England since Mary, Queen of Scots. Former landowners who had lost their positions and property thought that James would restore them to their former glory. James boosted these men's confidence when he appointed the earl of Tyrconnell, a Catholic, as his viceroy in Ireland.

To show James his support, Tyrconnell raised a Catholic army in Ireland. But Tyrconnell had misjudged—this wasn't the sort of support that James needed just then. The king's religion had made his reign shaky from the start. Anti-Catholic and anti-Irish sentiments were strong in England at that point, and an Irish-Catholic army was about the most alarming thing a good English Protestant could have imagined. Things went from shaky to really, really shaky, and in 1688 James fled to France.

# 49 } The Williamite War

Once James had run off, Parliament gave the crown to his Protestant daughter, Mary, and her husband, William of Orange, in what became known as the Glorious Revolution. It wasn't so glorious for Catholics, but it did result in the English Declaration of Rights—William and Mary had to grant their citizens certain basic rights if they wanted to remain on the throne. It was a crucial act in legal history.

In Ireland, however, people still supported James II. James borrowed an army from France's Louis XIV, a fellow Catholic, and sailed to Kinsale

Harbor in 1689. He joined up with Tyrconnell's Irish army and began to set up a power base from which he could regain the throne.

William, meanwhile, was skillfully working the European political scene. Once he'd promised to treat Ireland's Catholics well, he got the support of the Danes, Germans, and Dutch. Even the pope supported him; although popes had lobbied for a Catholic monarch in England for more than 100 years, Pope Alexander VIII was fighting against Louis XIV, so he opposed Louis's ally James as well.

King William III arrived in Ireland in 1690 with an international army of 36,000 soldiers. His forces swept through James's smaller Franco-Irish army at the Battle of the Boyne in July. James still had substantial resources that he could call up on his home territory, but he got spooked and fled to France again.

James's Catholic allies were left with the task of regrouping and facing William twelve months later at the Battle of Aughrim. This was another decisive victory for William.

The Irish army made its last stand at Limerick, but it had no chance of success. It sued for peace on the conditions that Catholics be spared religious persecution and that they have a guarantee of the same limited religious freedoms they'd had under Charles II. William agreed to the terms.

William did not stick to the terms agreed to at Limerick, however.

As soon as he didn't need his European allies, he rolled back all his promises. A new round of confiscations robbed Catholics of their land, and a series of penal laws imposed harsh restrictions on the civil and economic rights of Catholics. This period of Irish history is known as the Protestant Ascendancy.

While the Williamite victory marked a downfall in the status of Ireland's traditional population, it also initiated an era of peace. The 500-year period from the arrival of Strongbow to William's total victory was marked by constant warfare. The English conquered, the Irish lords fought to take their land back, and then the English returned to conquer again. The fighting only got more vicious once the Protestant Reformation added a religious element to the conflict. The preceding years of Viking conquests hadn't been terribly peaceful either.

It is fair to say, then, that the Protestant Ascendancy brought to Ireland a kind of peace and prosperity that it had never known. The shame is that the prosperity only applied to those at the top.

# 50 } Protestants Take Hold

During this period, the Anglican social elite dominated Ireland. They comprised about 25 percent of the population, but they owned most of the property and controlled law, politics, and society. For the island's native Catholic majority, however, it was a time of poverty and oppression.

The Treaty of Limerick of 1691 ended the violent wars that had ravaged Ireland in the seventeenth century. In the treaty, King William promised that Catholics would retain the right to practice their religion, and he gave the general impression that they would be treated fairly once they gave up their arms. Unfortunately, this proved not to be true. The king's true intention was to install a ruling class of Protestant landowners who would be loyal to the British Crown.

The victorious English government seized Catholic land to give to its Protestant supporters. The same thing had happened under the reigns of Elizabeth I, James I, and Cromwell. This time, however, the English were playing for keeps.

Members of the Protestant upper class had very mixed feelings about their new home and their place in it. Aristocrats who had moved from England felt as if they were living on a frontier, almost like colonists in the New World or in Africa. Some of them definitely didn't like Ireland and spent as little time there as possible; these were known as absentee landlords, who lived off the proceeds of Irish land and labor but contributed nothing themselves.

But Ireland simply wasn't the place to be if you wanted to further a career in England, and this frustrated many gentlemen. Jonathan Swift in particular hated living in Ireland. At the same time, he was quite conscious of the problems facing Ireland, most of which were brought on by its colonial status. The older he got, the more he identified with his adoptive homeland, and this was the inspiration for many of his more biting critiques, such as his "A Modest Proposal."

The now-Protestant Parliament enacted a series of infamous penal laws designed to limit Catholic power by curtailing Catholics' economic and social rights. Catholics were not allowed to bear arms, send their children to other countries for school, acquire land from Protestants, or make wills. Instead of deciding for themselves how their children would inherit, Catholics had to divide their property equally among all their sons, which resulted in increasingly small farms. There was an insidious catch, however—if the oldest son converted to the Protestant Church of Ireland, he inherited everything.

Irish clergy were expelled from the country. The Irish were not allowed to maintain schools, and in 1728 they lost the right to vote. All Irish culture and music was banned.

The penal laws didn't outlaw Catholicism, but they did make life very difficult for Catholics. The purpose of the laws was to keep Catholics from achieving enough wealth or legal power to challenge their Protestant rulers, and in that they were successful. It took more than 100 years before Catholics were able to mount any serious opposition to their subjugated state.

The penal laws didn't just hit Catholics; Ulster was home to a number of Scottish Presbyterians (the Scotch-Irish) who also refused to accept the strictures of the Church of Ireland, and they too lost a good deal of political power. When push came to shove, though, the Ulster Presbyterians generally joined forces with their fellow Protestants against the Catholics.

# 51 } Catholic Life

In response to the penal laws, a few of the educated folks converted to Protestantism and kept their jobs and property. Most Catholics, though, were forced to give up their lands and their careers and move. Thousands ended up in the south and west of Ireland, especially in rocky Connacht.

Peasants who had been property owners now had to rent property from local landlords. Leases were often short, as little as one year, which made it impossible for people to accumulate belongings or store food from year to year. Throughout the 1700s, periodic famines killed many poor people.

The Protestants took over most of the existing large churches, but that didn't prevent Catholics from hearing Mass. Priests performed Mass out in the open countryside on large, flat stones called Mass stones; the people would post lookouts to spot approaching armies and warn the participants in time for them to escape. This could be a dangerous business; tales from this period tell of the English hunting priests for sport or of ex-priests turning in their former colleagues to collect bounties.

As the 1700s wore on, the Protestants relaxed their enforcement of the penal laws. A Catholic middle class began to appear as Irish Catholics, forbidden from owning land, poured their energies into trade. Some of them were quite successful. As this happened, Protestants began to identify more with Catholics; they still didn't want to grant them equal rights, but they were united by their resentment of the British government.

Nevertheless, the penal laws were kept on the books; Protestants were only too aware that their property had originally been in Catholic hands, and they wanted to keep the laws even if they weren't often enforced. Irish Protestants were particularly worried that the British Parliament might one day cave in to Catholic pressure and change laws to Protestant disadvantage.

## 52 } The Second City of the British Empire

Dublin thrived in the eighteenth century, becoming the fifth-largest city in Europe. The ruling class supported arts and higher education and produced some of the most famous thinkers of the day.

The city of Dublin flourished during the Ascendancy. Aristocrats built themselves grand houses in the Georgian style. Urban planners designed a system of bridges and roads that allowed Dublin to expand into a city that stunned visitors from other countries who didn't expect to find urban grandeur in Ireland.

The stability of the 1700s allowed professional and intellectual societies to develop and the arts to flourish. The Dublin Society was founded in 1731 to encourage the arts, manufacturing, and agriculture; its members helped develop a distinctively Irish style of architecture and sponsored many large projects, such as botanical gardens and drawing schools. The Royal Irish Academy, founded in 1785, encouraged the study of Irish culture and history.

Many of Ireland's most beautiful country estates, gardens, and urban architecture date to the Protestant Ascendancy period. One impressive estate is Powerscourt House in Enniskerry, near Dublin (its famous gardens weren't built until the nineteenth century). Phoenix Park, opened in 1747, is one of the largest city parks in the world—more than twice as big as New York's Central Park. The Custom House, built in the 1780s, was the first major project of the famous architect James Gandon. He followed this project with designs for the Four Courts, consisting of the High Court and Supreme Court of Ireland. Gandon also had a hand in renovating the cupola of the spectacular Rotunda Hospital, opened in 1757 as Europe's first maternity hospital.

Trinity College came into its prime in the 1700s. Queen Elizabeth I founded it in 1592 to provide an institute of higher education for Protestants in Ireland; for most of its history, it has been completely Protestant. (Catholics were admitted in 1793, but it wasn't until 1970 that Catholics could enroll without being excommunicated from the Catholic Church; the majority of current students are Catholic.)

Many of the college's most important buildings were designed and built in the 1700s, including the Old Library, which now houses the *Book of Kells*. Trinity College was open to a variety of social classes; though everyone who went there was Anglican (and male), they were certainly not all noblemen. Many famous Irishmen of this period got their start there.

# 53 } Protestant Irish Nationalism

Once the Protestants had the Catholics under control, they started to examine their own situation vis-à-vis a larger power. Since Ireland had its own parliament, the Anglo-Irish questioned why the British Parliament had the right to pass legislation for Ireland.

The Protestants in Ireland began to see the Emerald Isle as their home, and they wanted it to be a nation distinct from Britain. Economics were a big concern; the British government regularly obstructed Irish economic development by restricting Irish trade. As Irish businessmen expanded their operations, they wanted to export their products, and British law often didn't allow that. Consequently, the Irish Protestants began to take a keener interest in the political process. This was the start of Protestant Irish Nationalism; its proponents became known as "patriots."

Now, the Irish Parliament, which the Normans brought to Ireland in the 1100s, was no paragon of democratic virtue. In the early eighteenth century, it consisted solely of members of the established Church of Ireland. The House of Lords was full of conservative bishops, and the House of Commons was composed of local clergy sent to Parliament on behalf of their wealthy patrons. Most of these men were more interested in feathering their own nests than in tackling constitutional issues, but at least they constituted a modicum of representational government independent of Britain.

The American War of Independence was bad news for British rule in Ireland. The Irish, both Catholic and Protestant, saw Britain's treatment of Ireland as analogous to its treatment of the American colonies, and they observed the American Revolution with keen interest. The American Declaration of Independence was greeted in Ireland with glee. The British responded by cracking down further on Ireland, trying to limit its trade with America.

In 1779, Henry Grattan, a young Irish Protestant, made a motion in Parliament to abolish the British restriction on Irish exports. He won this argument and proceeded to lead the Irish Parliament until the end of the century; the Parliament of this period is known as Grattan's Parliament.

Many Irish people, both Protestant and Catholic, were fully behind the Nationalist patriots. In the late 1770s, groups of Protestant men, known as Volunteers, joined the Irish cause—by 1779 there were Volunteers all over Ireland. Their main goals were to secure Irish free trade and to fight English interference with Irish government.

Grattan and other leaders realized they couldn't achieve independence from Britain without the help of the Catholic majority. So in 1778, Grattan pushed a Catholic Relief Act through Parliament; this act repealed some of the prohibitions on Catholic property ownership and inheritance. Grattan continued to rally his supporters and in 1779 won free trade rights for Ireland.

Pleased with his success, Grattan drafted an Irish declaration of independence in 1780. This measure passed in 1782 and gave Ireland the right to govern itself through its Parliament and judiciary. England still sent a viceroy to Dublin, and Dublin Castle was still answerable to the Crown, but it seemed to be a step forward.

The French Revolution, which began in 1789, gave more encouragement to Irish patriots; the Ulster Presbyterians were especially excited by the execution of Louis XVI and Marie Antoinette and the declaration of a French Republic. France seemed to be a model of religious tolerance, and the more idealistic Irish Protestant leaders accordingly decided that equality for Catholics would be good, or at least helpful to their cause.

## 54} Wolfe Tone's Rebellion

In 1791, a young Protestant named Theobald Wolfe Tone founded the Society of United Irishmen in Belfast. The United Irishmen's goal was to unite Irish people of all religions, to emancipate Catholics politically, to end the dominance of landlords, and to achieve political independence for Ireland. Wolfe Tone became secretary of the Catholic Association in Dublin, and through his efforts the Catholic population regained a number of the rights they had lost a century earlier. Catholic Relief Acts in 1792 restored the right to education, to practice law, to vote in local and parliamentary elections, and to bear arms. Catholics still couldn't sit in Parliament.

England didn't sit idle while this was going on. It formed a militia of citizens and passed the Convention Act to prevent public assemblies. In 1794 the British government repressed the United Irishmen in Dublin. The result was that the Irish people met in secret, and more of them began to agitate for more extreme reforms.

Wolfe Tone decided that the key to success was attracting the poor to his movement, and he emphasized the United Irishmen's commitment to protecting Catholics. Catholics were ready for action, and many joined his cause. But other Protestants weren't nearly as sure that they wanted to align themselves with Catholics. This tension was especially bad in the north, where Catholics had flocked in the wake of the new free-trade laws. Local Protestants feared Catholic competition in the profitable linen industry, and had been raised to fear Catholic theology as the teachings of the devil. The growing population didn't help, either, especially because Protestants saw Catholics as producing far more children than they did.

This tension found an outlet in secret agrarian societies, such as the Whiteboys or the Ribbonmen, which Catholics joined to protest unjust taxes or other points of contention; Protestants had their own groups. In South Ulster, the tension turned into a clear-cut conflict between Catholics and Protestants. Protestants in that area formed an armed group called the Peep O'Day Boys, and the Catholics responded with a group called the Defenders. These groups fought often; their most bloody battle was the 1795 Battle of the Diamond, in which the Protestants trounced the Catholics.

The victorious Protestants set up an organization called the Orange Order to protect their supremacy; they called themselves Orangemen, and many were government officials and leaders of the established church. The Catholics felt that the government was siding with the Orangemen and failing to protect them from Orange atrocities. This increasingly drove Catholics to side with Wolfe Tone and the United Irishmen, who were explicitly open to all religions and actively courted Catholic support.

In the second half of the 1790s, Wolfe Tone planned an armed rebellion against the English. He got to work drumming up military assistance for this enterprise, traveling to America and to France to rouse support for the Irish cause. His first efforts met with little success. In December 1796, he tried to land in Ireland with a group of French soldiers, but bad weather prevented his landing. The British government increased its repression of the United Irishmen; it had a network of spies that kept the authorities in Dublin Castle well informed of Irish movements.

Things came to a head in 1798. The United Irishmen had planned a huge rebellion in Dublin and had collected more than 20,000 pikes to use against British soldiers. Before they could get started, British troops marched into Dublin. They arrested the leaders of the Dublin United Irishmen and searched houses all over the city, turning up quite a pile of pikes.

Many Irish decided to go ahead with their rebellion and started small-scale efforts all over the country. They were poorly armed and disorganized without their leaders in Dublin, and the British quickly put them down. Between 30,000 and 50,000 Irish people rebelled, and many of them lost their lives. The French sent a small group of troops to Ireland to help the rebels, but they were quickly captured. Wolfe Tone was among them, dressed as a French officer; the British took him to Dublin and sentenced him to death, but he committed suicide in prison before he could be executed.

The British Parliament had no intention of letting Ireland rebel further. In 1800 they passed the Act of Union in both British and Irish

Parliaments, which created the "United Kingdom of Great Britain and Ireland." This act dissolved the Irish Parliament and instead created seats · for Irishmen in the British Parliament in London. In passing this act, Irish Parliament essentially voted itself out of existence.

The Act of Union polarized Protestant-Catholic relations by forcing Protestants to align themselves with Britain. It also paved the way for the career of one of the most important patriots in Irish history: Daniel O'Connell, also known as the Liberator.

## 55 } Hasta La Vista, Baby: Daniel O'Connell, the Liberator

O'Connell came from an aristocratic Catholic family in County Kerry. As a boy, he studied briefly at a hedge school, where he learned Gaelic history. He then went to school in France, where he observed the French Revolution firsthand; it's thought that the bloody events he witnessed there contributed to his avoidance of violence later in his political career. He was one of the first Irish Catholics to practice law after Catholics won back that right in the late 1700s.

O'Connell was strongly opposed to a union between Ireland and Britain. In 1823, he established the Catholic Association, a political organization whose goal was to force Britain's Parliament to admit Catholics. The association was open to all Catholics, rich or poor, and quickly became very popular. Even the poorest could afford the symbolic dues of one penny a month. O'Connell was a brilliant orator, and his followers loved his style and his rhetoric, in which he claimed that the poor would soon inherit the Earth. He promised that if the Act of Union were repealed, the Irish would have rent security, unjust rents would be ended, votes would become secret, more people would be allowed to vote, and landlords would be taxed to support the poor.

At this time, people who leased very small parcels of property (paying as little as £2 a year) were allowed to vote. Votes weren't secret, and landlords could and did "influence" the votes of their tenants. This meant that landlords had an interest in keeping lots of tenants on their land, because they could then control blocks of votes. The more tenants they had, the more votes they controlled.

Generally tenants complied with their landlords' wishes. But in 1826, encouraged by O'Connell, poor Catholics stood up to their landlords and elected to Parliament many legislators sympathetic to the Catholic cause. It was a start.

## 56  Catholic Emancipation

In 1828, O'Connell himself ran for Parliament as a representative from County Clare and won. This presented a problem for the British because, since the days of Queen Elizabeth I, anyone taking public or church office was required to swear an Oath of Supremacy, which acknowledged the British monarch as the head of church and state. Anyone who refused to take the oath could be charged with treason. Catholics who believed that the pope in Rome was the head of the Church obviously couldn't swear this oath, so it kept them out of office. But O'Connell called the British bluff; he refused to take the Oath of Supremacy, and Parliament capitulated by allowing him into office without it.

It did this by passing the Catholic Emancipation Act in 1829; this act allowed Catholics to enter Parliament and hold other important political offices without taking the oath. This accomplishment won O'Connell his famous nickname, the Liberator.

The Catholic Emancipation Act wasn't a perfect law; it mainly benefited the richer, middle-class Catholics. It actually made matters worse for the poor because it raised the rent requirement for voting to £10 a year. This disenfranchised most poorer property renters—now only about 1 percent of the Irish population could vote. It also took away any incentive landlords had to keep small tenants on their land and made the thought of using the land for profitable livestock more appealing. Landlords began getting rid of their tenants, which is one of the reasons the Great Famine was so devastating.

O'Connell's next goal was to get the Act of Union repealed, mainly so that the Irish Parliament could be reinstated. His poorer Irish compatriots wanted faster action than he could provide working in the British Parliament. They were disappointed that Catholic Emancipation hadn't been more profitable to them, and they began to take action for themselves.

O'Connell had kept agrarian secret societies, such as the Ribbonmen, quiet while he worked for emancipation, but now they rose up and again began to commit crimes against landlords. One continuing bone of contention was that Catholics had to pay tithes for the upkeep of Protestant clergy. In the 1830s, many Catholics refused to pay these tithes; this campaign became known as the Tithe War.

O'Connell kept working with the British Whig government to good effect. Through his efforts, Catholics won the right to be elected to important civic offices, and the Protestant Orange Order was quelled; the Orangemen didn't regain their strength until the 1880s. Tithes to the Church of Ireland were reduced, and some Poor Laws were passed to help the destitute. Most important for O'Connell, the Municipal Corporations Act of 1840 introduced more democratic local elections; as a result of this reform, O'Connell was elected mayor of Dublin.

These reforms were nice, but they didn't get to the root of Ireland's concerns—its continuing domination by the United Kingdom. In 1840, O'Connell founded the National Repeal Association, supported by the Catholic clergy and the Irish people. He declared 1843 "Repeal Year," and held "monster meetings"—huge and raucous gatherings—throughout Ireland to show the British government that he had ample support.

O'Connell's movement was undone by his insistence on nonviolence. The night before his last scheduled monster meeting, which was to have been held on the site of Brian Boru's famous victory at Clontarf, the British government made the gathering illegal, and O'Connell acquiesced rather than allow fighting to erupt.

That was the end of his great influence in Irish politics. His followers had seen him as a messiah, but now they felt that he had surrendered to the British. Many of them also disagreed with his insistence that Ireland was first and foremost a Catholic nation, arguing that politics should come before religion. These young men founded a new group, the Young Irelanders, which was to play an important political role in the second half of the nineteenth century.

Over a century and a half, from 1692 to 1840, Ireland lived through a time of unprecedented peace. There were no major wars, urban culture flourished, and high agricultural productivity led to a population boom. The positive aspects of the Protestant Ascendancy, however, could not cover up the fact that it was a society based on inequality and oppression. Resentment at this injustice flared up in the forms of Wolfe Tone's rebellion and O'Connell's independence movement. But true freedom was not to come about until after Ireland had endured its greatest tragedy—the Great Famine.

# PART 3

# Preserving Irish Culture and History

There can be no discussion of Ireland's history and culture without considering the role of the Roman Catholic Church. The Church has been integrated in Irish society for 1,600 years, and the word "Irish" has become almost synonymous with "Catholic." The Church has guided Irish nationalism and influenced the world's opinions of the Irish people, and it's still a major force in Ireland today.

## 57} Before the Reformation

In the Middle Ages (c. 500–c. 1500 C.E.), just about everyone in Ireland was Catholic, as was nearly everyone in England, Scotland, and Wales. At this time, almost all Western European Christians were Roman Catholic, led by the pope in Rome. Catholic churches were everywhere, in every town. Most people were baptized after birth, attended Mass, married in a church, and were buried in church cemeteries.

Saints were a very real presence, and believers prayed to them for help with their problems. Each saint had a different specialty; for example, someone with bad eyes would pray to St. Lucy, musicians would pray to St. Cecilia, and someone with a lost cause would pray to St. Jude for whatever help he could offer. The bones and physical possessions of saints supposedly could work miracles, and believers would travel to the places where these things were enshrined.

The liturgical calendar governed the course of the year. Each day was either an ordinary day or part of a ritual season like Lent or Advent. Every day had its own saint, which created a sort of family called the communion of saints. The liturgy was formulaic and ritualized and made it perfectly clear how a believer should worship.

On a local level, the Church was organized into geographical divisions called parishes, led by priests. Bishops oversaw larger territories that might encompass several parishes. A bishop had his seat in a cathedral.

Each parish priest oversaw the spiritual life of the people in his area, called parishioners.

Priests said Mass (in Latin, which most people didn't understand) and provided sacraments:

- ☘ Baptism—accepting a new member into the Church
- ☘ Penance—confessing sins to the priest, repenting, and being absolved
- ☘ Eucharist—the ceremonial re-enactment of the Last Supper
- ☘ Matrimony—the union of a man and a woman in marriage
- ☘ Extreme Unction—anointing of the sick and dying

Priests also ran schools, mediated quarrels, and helped the poor. In return, parishioners supported their priests with money and goods.

The Irish Church was run locally rather than externally, which made for lots of regional variation in practices. Outsiders tended to find Irish Catholicism both archaic and lax. Priests were respected, but they didn't control social structure; authority remained in the hands of chieftains and lords. The Irish mingled their Christianity with folk beliefs in fairies and changelings. Though the Catholic Church had decided in the eleventh century that its priests should be celibate, Irish priests continued to marry and have children. Divorce was allowed, and marriage between close relatives wasn't discouraged.

But however "unorthodox" their practices, the vast majority of Irish people were Catholic and knew it. They did not take it kindly when the English decided that they should change.

## 58 } Ireland's Counter-Reformation

Henry VIII's interest in Ireland (and in England) was primarily political, not theological, but subsequent monarchs became much more interested in what people believed. Queen Elizabeth I began a concerted effort to transform Ireland into a Protestant land. During her reign, Irish people were required to attend Anglican churches and use the Protestant Common Book of Prayer. Preaching in the Irish language was outlawed. A number of extreme Protestants called Puritans moved to Ireland. In the early seventeenth century, King James I sent many Protestant clergymen to Ireland and banished Catholic priests; he fined people who refused to attend Protestant worship services and banned Catholic school teachers. Priests were persecuted violently—some of them were drawn and quartered. But the Irish proved resistant to conversion. They refused to attend Protestant services and persisted in hearing Mass out in open fields.

When the Protestant Reformation began to gather steam, the Catholic Church set about creating its own institutional reforms, in an effort to revitalize itself and keep its members. The Council of Trent (1545–63) modernized the Church in Europe, but Ireland was slow to implement these modernizations.

The Pope watched the Reformation in England with great interest. He didn't want to lose Ireland, too. In 1606, the pope congratulated the Irish for sticking to their religion, and the Church leaders in Ireland decided it was time to modernize their parishioners.

The pope sent the Jesuits, a new group of Catholic missionary priests, to take on this project; the Jesuits found Irish Catholicism very strange. Not only was it full of odd Celtic rituals, the Irish Church itself was divided into an old Gaelic form, which rejected interference from Rome, and a (newer) Old English form, which embraced Roman doctrine.

The Jesuits worked on getting Irish priests to stop drinking and marrying, and encouraged the Catholic people to avoid Protestants. Although the Irish resisted change and persisted in holding their traditional wakes and casual marriages, the Catholic Church in Ireland did increase its presence and modernize some practices. The traditional Irish flexibility and adaptability proved useful in the survival of the institution.

In 1600, Ulster was a stronghold of rebel Catholicism, led by the prominent O'Neill family. Beginning in 1606, Scots were allowed to settle in Ulster as part of the Ulster Plantation plan. These settlers were predominantly Presbyterians who feared Catholics.

The English government encouraged this settlement because it helped them control Ireland economically and socially, as the settlers imposed "civilized" values on the Irish "barbarians." As English settlers continued to arrive in Ireland, they took much of the best farmland for themselves.

As a result, most Irish farmers and herdsmen saw their status continually diminished and deeply resented the occupiers.

The dispossessed O'Neills moved out into the hills and lived as outlaws, robbing and murdering travelers. They likened their Catholic troops to an army of Crusaders battling against the Turks, as they saw the Protestant invaders. This did not improve the Protestant opinion of them.

# 59 } Religious Tensions in the North

By the 1630s, the Catholics had regained much of their previous position in Ireland. Under King Charles I, they were allowed to worship fairly freely, they had reclaimed much of the land that had been taken away from them, and the number of Catholic priests had increased. But matters definitely were not peaceful.

The Protestant clergy resented the Catholic priests, who spoke Irish and were generally more popular with the Irish people. The Protestants thought the Catholic priests allowed the people to live in blind superstition. The Presbyterians in Ulster fervently believed that the Catholic Church was evil and its adherents idolatrous, and equated the pope with the anti-Christ. Groups of them swore to wipe out Catholicism. Ulster Catholics understandably felt threatened by this rhetoric.

Matters came to a head with the violent attacks of 1641, begun by the O'Neills as a political protest. Catholic leaders at home and abroad encouraged the rebels with the unfortunate suggestion that they kill the heretics or expel them from Ireland, which escalated the conflict into a bloody religious war.

The English Civil War began the following year, and the Irish Catholics supported King Charles. The Ulster Presbyterians supported Oliver Cromwell and the forces of Puritanism. Charles lost and was executed in 1649. Cromwell declared himself Lord Protector of England and immediately headed to Ireland, where he took revenge on the Catholics for supporting the king and for the violence of 1641.

Ulster Protestants were especially affected by the events of 1641 and were inclined to feel threatened by the Catholic presence. Because they were Presbyterian, they felt separate from the Anglican government as well and were never sure it wouldn't betray them; they resented any accommodation the government offered Catholics. This led to political separatism; as much as possible, the Ulster Protestants organized their own local government around their presbyteries.

Conservative Ulster Protestants were especially likely to evangelize and preach publicly. These preachers were extremely anti-Catholic and told their listeners stories of Catholic atrocities on Protestants. Protestants and Catholics were also separated economically—while the Protestants prospered through the linen industry, the Catholics were left out in the cold.

This combination of economic imbalance, social separatism, and Protestants' insecurity about their position has plagued Northern Ireland up to the present day. Protestants have long been the majority of the population, but they still aren't confident that Catholics will not be allowed to run roughshod over them. Even in the late 1990s, Protestants in Northern Ireland still claimed that the Roman Catholic Church was contrary to the word of God, or was equivalent to the Whore of Babylon, or wasn't Christian at all—rhetoric that hasn't changed much since the days of Cromwell.

The post-famine period in Ireland ushered in something of a devotional revolution. In the late 1840s, the number of priests and nuns increased dramatically at the same time that the general population was shrinking from death or emigration. The Church itself underwent major reforms.

Father Paul Cullen became archbishop of Armagh in 1849, at the end of the Great Famine, and he spent the next thirty years modernizing the Irish Church. He called the famine a work of God intended to purify the Irish people, whose Catholicism was too steeped in superstition and whose clergy was too tempted by avarice and sex; he also thought there were simply too many Catholics for the existing clergy to serve. He professionalized the clergy and introduced a variety of new rituals, including novenas, stations of the cross, parish missions, and adoration of the Blessed Sacrament. These changes brought the Irish Church more in line with Rome.

Post-famine Catholics became more devout than their ancestors had been, and Catholic priests had more power over them. People, especially in the eastern counties, enthusiastically joined new religious societies and embraced such devotional aids as the rosary, pilgrimages, shrines, processions, devotion to the Sacred Heart or the Immaculate Conception, and spiritual retreats. Older, "magical" events and events such as wakes, agricultural celebrations, and bonfires became less important.

## 60 } Modern Catholicism

These reforms also gave the Irish a new cultural identity by which they could recognize one another. The older Gaelic society was almost completely gone, and the Church offered a replacement social structure. It went without saying that a post-famine Irish person was also Catholic; the two were almost synonymous. Emigrant Irish took this cultural trait with them, and Irish all over the world were assumed to be devout Catholics.

This religious identity merged into the Irish national identity. For Irish farmers and laborers, Catholicism became synonymous with political freedom, rebellion against tyranny, and empowerment of the working classes.

The Catholic Church has remained powerful in Ireland throughout the twentieth century. It played a major part in the emergence of the Irish Free State and still dictates much of the structure of the Irish family. There are still churches everywhere in Ireland, and priests in them say Mass regularly.

Ireland is more strongly tied to Rome than many other Catholic countries in Europe. When Pope John Paul II visited Ireland in 1979, people traveled for days and camped out overnight in the hope of getting a glimpse of him. Irish Catholicism also has an extraordinary number of links to its Celtic and medieval past. Some religious holidays have direct links to pagan festivals; for example, the annual pilgrimage to Croagh Patrick originated in the Celtic festival of Lughnasa.

For most of the twentieth century, the Church controlled state-supported schools, which meant that almost all children were educated by priests, monks, and nuns. Some Irish remember the Catholic schools of their youth fondly. Others recall brutal physical punishments and being afraid to tell their parents for fear that their parents would beat them, too, so strongly did they believe in the Church's authority.

The Church has been present in family life as well. Irish often have crosses or religious pictures of the pope, Sacred Heart, or a favorite saint in their homes. Most Irish parents name their children after patron saints. Weddings and funerals almost invariably take place in the church; secular services are not popular. The Irish give more money to charity per capita than the people of any other European nation.

Up through the 1950s, many young Irish people chose religious vocations. Priests have long been honored and respected, and Irish priests have a reputation for being loving and devoted to their parishioners, though they can also be quite strict. Children and teenagers saw priests, monks, and nuns regularly, at church and at school, and the Church maintained a strong recruiting organization. Families who produced priests were praised, and many parents encouraged their children to seek a religious vocation. (Traditionally, it was a status symbol to have a priest or nun in the family, because it showed that the family had enough money to pay for religious education.)

The Church has played a very active role in modern Irish politics. The Irish Free State was set up in 1922 to be completely secular, but its leaders saw the Church as an Irish institution that distinguished them from the English. The Catholic archbishop Charles McQuaid of Dublin helped Éamon de Valera draft the constitution, which is explicitly Catholic. It guaranteed the Church a "special position" as the guardian of the faith of the majority of Irish citizens (the clause was removed in 1972). It also prohibited divorce and abortion and said in no uncertain terms that a woman's place was in the home.

# 61§ Scandals in The Church

The Church still has an extremely strong relationship with the government. Many Catholic voters insist that the government enforce their idea of what a family is. Ireland's leaders have therefore long kept very conservative views on issues such as contraception, abortion, divorce, and homosexuality.

Although the Catholic Church still plays a very important role for the Irish people, its power has been on the decline for decades. Fewer and fewer people now attend Mass. More significantly, the priesthood and the monastic vocations have lost much of their stature, thereby leading to a sharp drop in the number of people entering the religious orders.

The Irish Church has been plagued by some of the same sex-abuse problems that have shocked North American Catholics; the term "pedophile priest" has become disturbingly common. Irish Catholics have accused the upper levels of the Church hierarchy of attempting to cover up the scandals of accused clergy. The Christian Brothers organization, which runs several Irish schools, has publicly apologized for the many cases of abuse that occurred in its schools.

Birth control and abortion have generated some of the biggest debates in Ireland. For decades, the use of birth control was considered a criminal act. In 1950, a government health minister proposed a "Mother and Child" plan that would have put the state into the Church's traditional role of providing health care for pregnant women and mothers. Church leaders were afraid that the state might provide family-planning information, so they blocked the plan. The Church leaders got their way, but the resulting national controversy demonstrated that many Irish people were willing to challenge Catholic positions on social issues.

Between 1968 and 1993 the Irish Parliament passed a series of laws that made contraceptives legal and available. They did this in part with the support of the Irish people, partly because of pressure from the European Union to protect people's right to privacy, and partly to protect the population against sexually transmitted diseases. Church and conservative leaders opposed the new laws at every step, but the will of the people on this issue was clear. Abortion is still illegal, but thousands of Irish women travel overseas every year to terminate pregnancies.

Many young people in Ireland today feel alienated from the Church. They complain that the pope is too conservative and doesn't understand the needs of Catholic laypeople. They find that old-style Catholicism, with all its emphasis on shrines and the Virgin Mary, is irrelevant to modern people.

Ironically, though, one of the problems many modern Catholics have with the Church is that it has become too modern. The Second Vatican Council, convened by Pope John XXIII from 1962 to 1965, introduced a number of reforms into Church practice, including saying Mass in the vernacular and allowing laypeople to participate in Mass. Many Catholics had loved the old Latin Mass and the Gregorian chants in which it was sung and lamented its passing, as they did other forms of ritual that had been common and now are gone from Church practice. For some Catholics, that created a void that has not yet been filled.

## 62 } Traditional Irish Life

By the end of the seventeenth century, England's political domination of Ireland was complete. Although the English tried to force their language and religion onto Ireland, the Irish culture proved resilient. The Irish people continued to speak their language, play their music, and transmit their beliefs to their children.

There were great differences between the lifestyles of the Protestant Anglo-Irish ruling class and the Catholic Irish population. In Dublin and in their country estates, the Anglo-Irish gentry led lives very similar to their counterparts in England. The great mass of the Irish, however, led hardscrabble lives as small farmers and laborers.

Visitors to Ireland remarked on the obvious poverty of Irish farming families. Most families lived in small cottages, frequently with only one room and no floor. People wore simple clothes made of locally produced wool. Most heating came from peat, a brown substance from the bogs that burns for a long time but emits foul-smelling smoke. The diet of Irish farmers consisted of potatoes, milk, and a rare bit of meat.

The Irish exiled to Connacht had it particularly hard, because the rocky soil there is bad for farming. Their one blessing came from the abundant seafood in Irish waters. Fisherman would row out in *currachs* (COR-rahs), small boats made of pitch-coated cowhide stretched over a wooden frame. Fishing in these small craft was a dangerous business, but the seafood it produced added valuable protein and vitamins to the diet.

Despite the poverty that most of the Irish experienced, they still managed to have fun. Through their language, music, dancing, and sports, they were able to express themselves in distinctively Irish ways.

## 63 } Irish Language

The Gaelic language of Ireland is one of the most distinctive in Europe. It's one of the few Celtic languages that survived the onslaught of Germanic and Latin tongues. Some of the oldest vernacular literature in Europe was composed in Irish, and an extraordinary range of Irish stories survived into the modern day. Irish is a lyrical language that seems particularly well suited to poetry and metaphor. But it's lucky to be around today. We have the efforts of many generations of stubborn Irish people to thank for its modern existence.

In 1500, the great majority of Ireland's inhabitants still spoke Irish as their first language. The Anglo-Norman families like the FitzGeralds and Butlers spoke both English and Irish, but the farmers and laborers outside the Pale spoke predominantly Irish. With the plantations and conquests of the sixteenth and seventeenth centuries, however, the language trends began to change.

Thousands of English-speaking families moved onto Irish land. English policies actively promoted the adoption of the English language. There's a story that schoolteachers would hang sticks from students' necks and notch them every time they spoke Irish; for every notch the student would receive a beating. The most powerful force against Irish was the fact that all the wealthy and powerful people spoke English, so a person needed to speak English to have any opportunities for advancement. Between

1700 and 1900, Irish went from being the majority language of the island to a minor tongue spoken by disenfranchised groups in the West.

While the Irish were pressured to speak English, it was hard for them to learn to read it. The penal laws prevented most Irish children from attending school. But the Irish had a resourceful response to this problem; they created hedge schools—informal schools taught in the open or in barns by volunteer schoolteachers. These schools taught English, Irish, Latin, history, geography, and whatever else they could manage. They didn't have many books and couldn't meet all the time, but they did prevent the Irish people from becoming totally illiterate.

Although it suffered, the Irish language didn't die out. It lived on in remote places with little English presence, particularly in the West. The English didn't bother to put schools in backward outposts like the Blasket Islands off the Dingle coast. The province of Connacht, which Cromwell had seen fit to leave to the Irish, remained the bastion of the old Gaelic language. The area where Irish continued to be spoken as a first language was called the Gaeltacht.

Over the years, the Irish government has instituted a number of programs to preserve the Irish language. Irish is the official language of the Republic of Ireland and a mandatory part of the curriculum for all Irish schoolchildren. For a while, all civil servants had to pass examinations in Irish before they could take their posts. The government has provided a number of incentives to promote Irish-language initiatives in the Gaeltacht, such as Raidió na Gaeltachta, an all-Irish radio station.

# 64 } Irish Music

There has been a major upsurge of interest in traditional Irish music in recent years. Bands like The Chieftains and Clannad have helped develop a worldwide interest in the lyrical sound of Celtic music. Musicians throughout Ireland and its emigrant communities have found opportunities to play for adoring crowds in Irish pubs everywhere. These musicians are continuing in a Celtic music tradition that goes back many centuries.

Poets and bards were big shots in Celtic societies. A good poet could grant either fame or shame to Celtic nobles, so when one showed up at court and started to sing, everyone gathered to listen. These bards often played harps and other musical instruments. Brian Boru's harp—the symbol of Ireland—was supposedly played to rally his troops.

The singing poets continued their cultural influence after the Norman Conquest. The Anglo-Norman nobles, like the old Irish nobles before them, recognized the power of a good song, so they often sponsored these bards in their courts. Over time, however, the power of the bards waned. With books and letters available, nobles no longer needed poets to spread their fame.

Irish music is a free-form style. The length, pace, and musical composition of a given piece will change from night to night and from group to group. Traditional musicians almost never play from written music; in the past, many of the best musicians couldn't even read music. As in American jazz, most pieces revolve around group performances that highlight the virtuosic improvisations of individual musicians.

Despite the free-form style, Irish music has a distinctive sound that makes it immediately identifiable (although Scottish and Welsh music sound similar). The distinctiveness comes largely from the mix of instruments used. The traditional instruments of Irish music are:

- Harp
- Bodhrán drum
- Fiddle
- Flute
- Tin whistle
- Accordion
- Bagpipes or uilleann pipes
- Pretty much anything that can jam

Traditional music performances are informal. They generally take place in pubs, with the musicians performing only for free beer and the cheers of the crowd. Members of the audience can join in if they have a fiddle, a good voice, or even just a set of spoons to add to the music.

The Irish love of poetic language mixed with humor and tragedy to produce the beautiful Irish ballad. The ability to compose and perform a beautiful ballad has been highly prized in Ireland for centuries. The ballad is generally sung by a single person, who may or may not be accompanied by instruments. Ballads range from a handful of lines to many hundreds of lines in length. They can tell stories of lost love, injustice and revenge, or what happened when the singer went to get a beer.

# 65 } Before There Was Riverdance . . .

Dancing has been an important form of artistic expression and social interaction in Ireland for thousands of years. The Celts and the druids had their own forms of folk dancing. Some say that the prevalence of ring structures in modern Irish dancing has to do with the way the ancient druids danced around sacred oak trees—either that, or it's just easier to dance in a circle.

The Vikings, the Normans, and the English all probably contributed to the development of dance in Ireland. By the sixteenth century, three dances were spoken of as distinctively Irish: the Irish Hey, the Rinnce Fada, and the Trenchmore. Sir Henry Sidney, Queen Elizabeth's lieutenant in Ireland, saw some comely Irish lasses dancing Irish jigs in Galway. He wrote, "They are very beautiful, magnificently dressed and first class dancers." Whenever royalty or important guests visited Ireland, it was customary to meet them with fancy dancers.

The steps toward the development of contemporary Irish dance are unclear. It is known, however, that dancing was an important part of the social lives of the native Irish population. Festivals, weddings, and wakes were all occasions for dancing. Towns would have dance competitions, and wandering dance masters would go from town to town, teaching all the latest steps. It was through the influence of these itinerant masters that the Irish forms of the jig, reel, hornpie, and polka developed.

Today, thanks in part to Riverdance, Irish step-dancing is the most recognizable form of Irish dance. In this style, dancers hold a rigid posture, keep their arms mostly by their sides, and step and kick about for all they're worth. Many Irish dancers maintain that their ancestors developed this rigid-armed style of dancing so that if English people looked in through a window they wouldn't be able to tell that the Irish were dancing. There may be a grain of truth to this, but most dance scholars think that the style was adapted from French dances imported in the eighteenth century.

The most authentically Irish form of dance is the *céilí*, or *ceilidh* (kaylee), which is similar in form to folk dancing in many other parts of the world. A *céilí* is essentially a dance party in which everyone dances to traditional Irish music, spinning, exchanging partners, waltzing around, and generally having a good time. *Céilí* dance arrangements generally involve four or more dancers at a time. Irish-American organizations throughout the United States host *céilís* from time to time.

## 66 } Death and the Supernatural

For the Irish, a funeral isn't just an occasion for mourning. It is also an opportunity to get together with friends, meet members of the opposite sex, and play wild games. This both honors the dead person and allowed the living to rejoice in their continuing life.

Traditionally the corpse and his or her family would be separated from the party by a screen so that the mourners could grieve and weep without distraction. Meanwhile, all the guests would drink whiskey, sing, smoke, and play various party games. These games involved mock marriages and some games that the clergy condemned as downright obscene—not unlike the games played at some teenage parties today. Flirtation was allowed but fornication was not; the Irish did not approve of sex outside of marriage.

The Irish people have maintained a set of unique beliefs and superstitions that have lived on until the modern day. There is an abundance of stories and superstitions about the mischief of the fairies. The Irish term for the fairies is *sídhe* (shee); in English they are called by a number of terms, such as "wee folk" or the "good people." Irish legends suggest that there is an extraordinary diversity of charming and terrifying fairies frolicking in the countryside:

- **Changelings**—fairy children left in place of stolen mortal babies; the fairies were said to leave sickly babies after stealing healthy ones.
- **Bean sídhe** (banshee)—a female spirit associated with the ancestors of old Irish families, who wails terribly whenever someone in the family dies.

- **Gruagach**—a female spirit that guards livestock but requires an offering of milk.
- **Selkies**—gentle spirits that are seals by day but humans by night; they sometimes marry human fishermen.
- **Lianhan shee**—a sort of love goddess who invites men for trysts in Tír na nÓg (the home of the fairies); loving the Lianhan shee almost invariably results in disaster.
- **Leprechauns**—short, mischievous creatures known for their skills in making shoes and hiding gold; if a mortal traps one at the end of a rainbow, he can take his pot of gold.
- **Cluricauns**—similar to leprechauns, except they don't make shoes and they like to steal shepherds' dogs and goats for impromptu midnight races.
- **Pooka**—a spooky spirit who appears as a black eagle, goat, or horse; he has the irritating habit of picking up unwary travelers for terrifying midnight rides, sometimes into the sea.

It is widely suspected that the fairies came from one of the races that inhabited Ireland before the Celts arrived. There is an abundance of rings of stones throughout the Irish countryside. Local legend generally attributes these "fairy rings" to Ireland's mystical inhabitants from the past. Superstitious locals have avoided the rings for centuries. Less superstitious archaeologists usually attribute the rings to Ireland's Stone Age inhabitants.

The beauty of Irish superstitions is that the Irish adopted all the superstitions of Christian culture without giving up their old Celtic beliefs. The result was a whole cornucopia of beliefs about how to avert disaster, placate the fairies, or attain wealth and love.

A great many superstitions dealt with relations with the spirit world. The wee folk were notoriously mischievous, so a wise person kept a number of practices in mind—only calling them "the good people," for example. People called out a warning whenever they threw water out of the house, for fear of hitting an unsuspecting fairy. To stay on the fairies' good side, sensible housewives always left out little plates of food or milk for the little people to enjoy. If someone should be so unfortunate as to cross paths with hostile fairies, it was well known that throwing dust from under one's feet would force the fairies to give up any human captives. When gathering wood for a fire, people would never take anything growing on a fairy mound.

A number of beliefs dealt with specific holidays. On Halloween it was customary to put up Parshell crosses—two sticks tied together with twine—to keep spirits at bay (the Parshell cross looks suspiciously like the spooky sticks in the film *The Blair Witch Project*). On May 1, a woman could achieve great beauty by rolling naked in the morning dew. St. Stephen's Day—December 26—was also known as Wren Day because local boys would hunt down a wren and then parade it around town on a stick for good luck. On Whit Sunday it was considered unwise to go anywhere near water, because it was widely known that the spirits of drowned people would rise up on that day and try to pull down the living.

# 67} IRISH SPORTS

The Celts were an active, warlike folk, so when they found themselves at peace, they invented warlike sports to keep themselves fit. Although they'd beaten their Celtic swords into plowshares, Irish farmers continued to play these exciting sports. In the late nineteenth century, the Gaelic Athletic Association (GAA) officially revived them. GAA matches still gather roaring crowds from across the island.

One of the most unique Irish sports is hurling, an ancient game played by two fifteen-member teams armed with curved wooden sticks called "hurlies." They use the sticks to smack around a hard leather ball (*sliothar*), at speeds of up to 80 miles per hour, until it goes through a hoop. With all the swinging and smacking, injuries are common; it's said that the ancient Celts used the sport as a training tool to give their warriors strong bones. The All-Ireland Hurling Final, held every year at Croke Park in Dublin, excites fanatical enthusiasm.

The woman's version of hurling is called *camogie*. *Camogie* matches tend to be somewhat less violent than the men's matches, but they are popular anyway.

Hurling is an ancient sport, and forms of it have evolved into a number of popular modern sports. The Scottish form of hurling is called *shinty*. Since *shinty* involves hitting a ball around with a stick, it is thought to have inspired that other Scottish sport, golf. Hurling and *shinty* enthusiasts who emigrated to Canada, adapted their favorite sport to the ice and called it hockey. Unlike the Celts or the Irish, however, the Canadians had the sense to wear pads.

A marginally safer form of hurling evolved into Gaelic football, the GAA's other major sport. It's kind of like soccer, except the players use their hands, and it's kind of like rugby, and the players don't wear pads. Games are fast and furious.

## 68 } Rich Folklore and Heritage

Irish storytellers are famous for their wit and inventiveness. The extraordinary range of Irish stories comes from a folklore tradition more than 2,000 years old, which successfully blended Celtic, Christian, and English influences to create some of the most distinctive oral literature in all of Europe. Although the traditional format for Irish storytelling is dying out, its legacy continues in books and in poetry.

Ireland has one of the richest folklore traditions in the world. Folklorists have hypothesized that in 1935 the parish of Carna, in west Galway, held more unrecorded folktales than did the rest of Western Europe combined. There are many reasons for this rich heritage, but two main factors stand out. First, Irish culture kept a Celtic base for more than 2,000 years, while incorporating the traditions and beliefs of Christianity, the Vikings, the Normans, and the English. These layers of culture piled on top of one another to create a rich tapestry. Second, the tradition of oral composition and performance has been strong in Ireland throughout the years.

In ancient Celtic society, professional singers and poets called bards were extremely important. The Celts didn't write, so bards memorized vast amounts of poetry and performed it live. Their poems and songs were often the only record of a king's deeds or misdeeds, and their performances were the best entertainment around. People were accustomed to listening to stories told aloud and appreciated skilled storytellers.

As time went on, more people learned to read and write and the bards became less important. But the Irish populace remained mostly illiterate, so they kept up the tradition of oral storytelling. Bards evolved into wandering storytellers called *shanachies*, or *seanachai* (SHAN-uck-ee), who went from town to town, entertaining the townsfolk. *Shanachies*, like their bard predecessors, were always welcome; people paid them with food if money wasn't available. When there wasn't a *shanachie* around, ordinary people entertained themselves by telling stories around the fire.

A good storyteller knew hundreds of tales and could perform them with gusto and eloquence. In this informal way, an ancient oral literary tradition quietly continued into modern times.

For centuries, Irish folktales were unknown to the outside world. During the Protestant ascendancy, the ruling class had nothing but disdain for the stories of Irish farmers. Not only were the stories in the barbaric Irish tongue, but also they were all about fantastic heroes and fairies, which the English dismissed as a bunch of superstitious nonsense.

In the early nineteenth century folklore suddenly became fashionable. The brothers Grimm in Germany started collecting and studying folktales (which you can read in *Grimm's Fairy Tales*) and declared folklore a vital expression of a culture's heritage. Soon, enterprising Irish scholars began to explore the countryside, looking for stories of value. They found a gold mine.

The first volume of Irish folktales was *Fairy Legends and Traditions of the South of Ireland*, published in 1825 by Thomas Croker from Cork. Croker and other early scholars of Irish folklore visited the Anglicized areas of Ireland in the east and recorded stories in English; this limited the value of their work because it ignored the great majority of Irish folktales, which were told only in Irish. In the mid-nineteenth century, Jeremiah Curtin, an Irish-American who had learned Irish, traveled throughout the Irish-speaking enclaves in Connacht and discovered hundreds of previously unrecorded stories. He recorded them in their original language and greatly advanced the study of Irish folklore.

At the end of the nineteenth century, Irish folklore studies became respectable. Oscar Wilde's parents, Sir William and Speranza Wilde (Speranza was Mrs. Wilde's pen name, her real name was Jane Francesca), were important figures in this field and eccentric luminaries on the Anglo-Irish scene. The intellectuals of the Celtic Renaissance drew their inspiration from the Irish language and its folklore. Douglas Hyde's *Beside the Fire*, William Butler Yeats's *The Celtic Twilight*, Lady Augusta Gregory's *Visions and Beliefs of the West of Ireland*, and Standish O'Grady's collections not only established Irish folklore as one of the great oral literature traditions of Western civilization, but also provided an immense source of pride for the growing Irish Nationalist movement.

Even as Yeats and Lady Gregory collected tales in the cottages of Sligo and Connemara, they recognized that the storytelling tradition was dying out. They knew that if the Irish language died, a vast literary heritage would die with it. To prevent that from happening, in 1935 the Irish government created the Irish Folklore Commission. In the following decades, Irish-speaking collectors scoured the countryside to record stories of saints, heroes, and spirits. Currently, more than a million and a half pages of folklore reside in the commission's collection which, since 1971, has been continued on by the Folklore Department at University College Dublin.

One of the most popular themes for stories was the spirit world. Ireland was widely known to be inhabited by all manner of fairies. The fairies were notoriously mischievous, and a vast array of stories described the mysterious tricks they played on unsuspecting mortals.

The leprechaun is perhaps the most famous of Ireland's little people. In one story, a man came down from his fields one day and went to look after his old mare, who had served him well for many years. When he approached the stable, he heard a loud hammering sound. He peeked in through a window and spotted a funny little man sitting under his mare, hammering away at some shoes and whistling the prettiest tune you ever heard. The man realized what he had in his stable—a leprechaun.

Leprechauns are famous for their shoemaking abilities, but they're even more famous for their gold. The man knew this, so he snuck in the backdoor and tiptoed up behind the little man. The leprechaun was so busy making his shoes that he didn't notice the man until the man had caught the leprechaun fast. "I have you now," the man said, "and I won't let you go until I have your gold!"

"Stop, you're squeezing too hard!" said the leprechaun. "Let me go for a moment and I'll get you the gold." Eager for the gold, the man released the leprechaun, who, quick as a wink, ran out the door. All the man had left was the little shoe that the leprechaun had been making. The man didn't get any gold, but his wife said that it was the prettiest shoe she'd ever seen.

Some fairies were thought to be helpful, in their own mysterious ways. One story tells of a man who started feeling faint while in church. He walked outside to clear his head, and a gentleman approached to ask if he was all right. The man explained that he was feeling faint. The gentleman handed him a florin (a valuable coin) and told him to go have a whiskey at the local pub (Irish whiskey, of course, has amazing curative powers). The man thanked him and walked to the pub.

He paid for his drink with the florin, took the change, and drank down the whiskey. In no time at all he was feeling better. The man went home thinking nothing of it.

The next day he was going fishing, so he went to the store to buy some tobacco for his trip. When he reached into his pocket to get some money, he was surprised to find that the same florin was in his pocket. He paid with the florin, took the change, and walked away smoking, wondering what had happened. On the way home after fishing, he stopped by the bakery for some bread. He discovered that the same florin was in his pocket again.

The man continued in this way for some time, paying for everything with the florin and always finding it back in his pocket. He was happy with his good fortune, but something about the strange coin never seemed right to him. One day he went into the pub where he'd bought the first glass of whiskey. He threw the florin down on the counter and yelled, "May the devil go with you!"

He never saw the coin again. To the end of his days, he always said that it was a fairy man who had given it to him.

## 69 } Potatoes, for Better or Worse

An Gorta Mór, the Great Potato Famine of the 1840s, is one of the pivotal events in Irish history. Millions emigrated, and the resulting demographic shift led to a decreasing population. The famine also ignited anger at the British government, which eventually grew into the Irish independence movement.

Potatoes came to Europe from the New World in the early sixteenth century. Sir Francis Drake is thought to have introduced the potato to England, and shortly afterward Sir Walter Raleigh tried planting them on his Irish estates.

When potatoes reached Ireland, they created a revolution. They were very easy to grow; farmers could plant them in the spring and leave them alone for months while they went off and worked elsewhere (anywhere that scarce wages might be offered). People grew potatoes on any patch of land that could sustain them, even the most marginal of fields.

Potatoes are extremely nutritious; they are full of vitamins, protein, calcium, and iron, especially when washed down with buttermilk, the potato's traditional accompaniment. The potato, in fact, is perhaps the only crop that can provide a balanced diet by itself, which kept the Irish healthier than other people living on one starch such as rice or millet or even bread (made of wheat). It was relatively easy to store over the winter, which was important because most tenant farmers had no buildings in which to store vast quantities of grain. Unfortunately, you can't store potatoes for much more than a year, and this would have devastating consequences for the Irish in the famine years.

Patterns in land ownership made Irish farmers dependent on the potato. Most farmers had to rent from landlords (who were usually English) who demanded cash payments. The farmers had to use most of their time and land to produce cash crops to cover the rent, and consequently they only had small amounts of time or land left to grow their own food. Given these constraints, the potato was the only crop that could provide sufficient nutrition to feed the growing Irish families.

And grow they did; between 1700 and 1800 the population doubled from somewhere around 2.5 million people to about 5 million people.

By the early 1840s, the population stood at 8.2 million; ironically, it was densest in the poorest areas. The potato helped make this possible, but population growth also made people more dependent on the potato. Fathers would split up their land between their sons, making families depend on smaller and smaller plots of land. The system worked, but only as long as the potatoes were plentiful.

So there the Irish were, planting their potatoes every spring, digging them up every fall, and eating rather well, all things considered. But in the autumn of 1845, all that changed.

In October of that year, farmers walked out to their fields to harvest their crops. They plunged their shovels into the ground and then shrieked in horror—the potatoes were black and rotten, completely useless. The crop they had counted on for generations had finally failed them.

No one knew what to do. Experts offered advice, suggesting that the fungus killing the potatoes was attracted to moisture. Farmers tried to dig dry pits, but the spores traveled through the air and soaked into the ground after rain, which has always been plentiful in Ireland. It took only one infected plant to spread the blight over acres of potatoes. There was no escape.

The west and southwest of Ireland bore the brunt of the famine. Those areas, including Mayo, Sligo, Roscommon, Galway, Clare, and Cork, were the poorest regions of the island, and the most dependent on subsistence farming. Not coincidentally, these were also the areas that Catholic Irish had been sent to during the Protestant plantation. Poor laborers were hardest hit, followed by the smallest farmers.

The worst part of the potato blight was that it didn't go away. After the 1845 crops failed, people counted on the potatoes of 1846 to pull them through, but those potatoes rotted away, too. For some reason the crop of 1847 survived, but not enough fields of potatoes had been planted to produce enough food for everyone who needed it. And in 1848 the blight reappeared with a vengeance.

# 70 } LIFE DURING THE FAMINE

The poor Irish who had lost their potatoes faced terrifying difficulties. They called the time an Gorta Mór, which means "the Great Hunger," or an Droch Shaol, "the Bad Times."

The poorest farmers, already living at a subsistence level, were the first to feel the effects. Within a few months of the bad harvest, the people in the hardest-hit areas were already dying of starvation. Travelers reported seeing skeletal people with their mouths stained green; they had tried to ward off hunger by eating grass. In some places in western Ireland, piles of corpses filled the ditches.

The first thing the stricken farmers did was try to eat their diseased potatoes. This made them terribly sick with stomach cramps, diarrhea, and intestinal bleeding. Some very old and very young people died from this disease.

There was some food to be found on the land, and the Irish were very resourceful at scrounging it. They trapped birds and stole eggs from nests, gathered shellfish from the shores, and caught fish. Coastal people ate seaweed. They would take blood from cattle and fry it. They ate rats, worms, nettles, and chickweed. When the opportunity presented itself, they stole food from wagons and barges. But none of it helped much.

The malnourished Irish were very vulnerable to diseases. In fact, more people died from illness than from actual starvation.

Typhus appeared in the winter of 1846. The Irish called it the black fever because it made victims' faces swollen and dark. It was incredibly contagious, spread by lice, which were everywhere. Many people lived in one-room cottages, humans and animals all huddled together, and there was no way to avoid lice jumping from person to person. The typhus bacteria also traveled in louse feces, which formed an invisible dust in the air. Anyone who touched an infected person, or even an infected person's clothes, could become the disease's next victim. Typhus was the supreme killer of the famine; in the winter of 1847, thousands of people died of it every week.

Another fever appeared at the same time, the relapsing fever called yellow fever because its victims became jaundiced. This fever also came from lice. A victim would suffer from a high fever for several days, seem to recover, and then relapse a week later. Many people died from this fever as well.

Scurvy became a problem. This disease comes from a deficiency of vitamin C, and it causes the victim's connective tissue to break down. The Irish called scurvy black leg, because it made the blood vessels under the skin burst, giving a victim's limbs a black appearance. The cure for scurvy is fresh food—meat, vegetables, or fruit—none of which was available to the poor in Ireland.

There were other diseases, too. Some Irish children fell victim to an odd disease that made hair grow on their faces while it fell out of their heads. Some observers commented that the children looked like monkeys. Cholera was always a problem in unsanitary, crowded conditions; it broke out in workhouses throughout the famine years.

When people died, the living were left with the problem of what to do with the bodies. There were not enough coffins to hold the dead, even if the poor had money to pay for them. Stories abounded of entire families dying, or of mothers losing all their children and carrying the bodies to the cemetery on their backs, one by one. Visitors reported seeing dead bodies stacked in ditches and dogs devouring corpses in the fields; to their horror, they also observed people killing and eating those same dogs.

When someone came down with typhus, relatives and neighbors feared that they would contract the disease, too. Sometimes all healthy members of a family would leave a sick person alone in a house, hoping to escape the contagion. They hadn't abandoned the sufferer; they would push food in through the windows on the end of a long pole. When there was no longer a response from inside the house, they would pull the house down on top of the victim and burn the whole thing.

Most of the victims of the famine did not own the land they lived on. Instead, they rented houses and farmland from large landholders. When the potato crops failed, they could no longer pay their rent. Some landlords were understanding; many actually helped their tenants, handing out food and concocting jobs that would allow them to earn wages.

But other landlords were less accommodating. Scores of poor Irish were evicted from their homes. This wasn't all due to cruelty and greed; many landlords themselves faced bankruptcy and starvation as their rents stopped coming in. Some landlords decided that grazing sheep or cattle would be a better use of the land, and the peasants and their potato plots had to give way for the livestock.

The result was that many poor Irish found themselves not only starving, but homeless as well. Some of them moved into workhouses, but many dug holes in hillsides or made huts out of peat and lived in them as best they could. Others simply wandered the roads until they dropped dead.

# 71 } Help! Responses to the Famine

One of the things that made the Irish famine especially bad was a lack of help for the starving. The British government was reluctant to help too much, partly out of fear that the poor would depend on aid and not try to help themselves. The mid-nineteenth century was the heyday of laissez-faire economics, which taught that the free market would solve all problems and that the government should never intervene. Unfortunately, that approach led to tragedy for the Irish population.

Politicians quickly got word that the Irish peasantry had nothing to eat. Many English were not particularly impressed with the Irish plight.

A number of them thought that the famine was a punishment for Ireland's sin of overpopulation. According to population theorist Thomas Robert Malthus, Ireland had far too many people for its land to support, and the best solution was to get rid of most of them. The famine would take care of that.

The truth was, the factors that contributed to the Irish famine were far more complex than mere overpopulation. There was plenty of food in Ireland. The island grew and exported more than 1 billion pounds of grain every year. Many Irish actually sold this food willingly so they would have the money to pay rent. Ireland also was not allowed to import rice or corn from the British colonies. This was the effect of the Corn Laws (the British call wheat "corn"; they call corn "maize"), which set artificially high prices for British grain and locked out cheaper imports until the entire British crop was sold. This was a problem for the Irish, who had no money.

Prime Minister Robert Peel initially took pity on the starving Irish, and, unbeknownst to his own government, ordered Indian corn from the Americas to be delivered to the island. This corn was only a last resort for the sufferers; it was difficult to grind and cook, not nearly as filling as potatoes, and it lacked vitamin C. It ran out quickly, too, and was not replaced.

Peel resigned in 1846, and for the next four years the man he appointed to oversee famine relief, Charles Edward Trevelyan, handled matters. Trevelyan didn't have a very high opinion of the Irish, and in fact only visited Ireland once; he thought distance helped him maintain objectivity. He was a firm believer in laissez faire and thought donated food actually exacerbated the problem by relieving the Irish of the obligation to feed themselves. Unfortunately, in some places, no one had either food or money, so feeding themselves was completely impossible. Irish crops continued to be exported, which led to great resentment on the part of the Irish people.

When people got truly desperate, there was a place that they could go: the workhouse. These houses had been established in the early 1840s to provide relief to the poorest people. Opponents of workhouses feared that the Irish would abuse the system, using the workhouse if they weren't truly desperate. But supporters countered that they could solve this problem by making workhouses so unpleasant that only people with no alternative would enter them.

Unpleasant they were. Anyone who owned land had to give it up before entering a workhouse, which forced many families to choose between staying on their farms and starving or giving up their land for a chance to eat. People who entered a workhouse were segregated by sex, which meant dividing up families. They were forced to live there, essentially sentencing themselves to prison. They had to give up their own clothes and wear pauper's uniforms, which marked them as destitute. They had to work at menial jobs to earn their keep—men broke up rocks, women knitted, and children either had lessons or learned to do various industrial tasks. Families only got together on Sundays.

The Irish people did everything they could to avoid the workhouse. They found the splitting up of families especially hard to bear. The unpleasant regimen did succeed in keeping people away from public charity in the early 1840s and even into 1846, before the second bad potato crop.

But after the second nonexistent potato harvest in the autumn of 1846, people were more willing to surrender their dignity in the hopes of not starving. Poorhouse food was bad and often inadequate, but at least it was food. By mid-October, most workhouses in the worst-hit areas were full and turning away inmates.

Crowding did nothing to improve the workhouse atmosphere. The stench became overpowering as hundreds of unhealthy people contributed their bodily products to the building. Typhus, cholera, and other diseases thrived in this environment, and many people died.

Not everyone could fit into the workhouses, and many people refused to even consider the possibility. The government provided an alternative for them: working for pay on public projects. Local relief committees made lists of people who needed help, and then one member of each needy family was allowed to work for pay.

This was a nice idea, but ineffective in practice. The projects in question involved hard physical labor—digging ditches, breaking and moving rocks to build roads—and the workers were already malnourished. The winter of 1846 to 1847 was especially harsh, and the workers had no adequate clothes. Many of them fell sick and dropped dead on the job. In fact, 1847 was such a bad year that it became known as Black '47.

The wages for public works would have been generous in the days of plentiful potatoes, but during the famine food prices went through the roof. A week's wages were barely adequate to buy half a week's sustenance for a family of any size, and many Irish families were large. Families were desperate to keep someone on the works to collect money, though, so they would often deprive nonworkers of food to keep up the strength of the wage-earner. Children would go hungry so their father could eat.

In many cases, the person going out to work was also the person who would have planted the next year's potato crop at home. Without that labor, the next year's harvest suffered.

At the start of the famine, the government insisted that charity was best done by private institutions. The Quakers in particular rose to the occasion, opening soup kitchens to feed paupers. Some landlords helped their tenants, providing food, clothes, or housing. Irish peasants helped one another when they could; many stories from the famine years tell of housewives who gave away their last cabbage in the garden or last drop of milk from the cow, only to have their supplies miraculously renewed the next morning. These are nice stories, but unfortunately usually not true.

In 1847, the government stopped the public-works programs and announced that from now on, private aid would be the solution. The British still feared that too much aid to the Irish would prevent them from ever going back to work. The British decided that Irish landlords must be responsible for the famine, so it would be their job to fix it. Local governments were supposed to organize charitable soup kitchens paid for by taxes collected by local relief committees.

But as the famine years progressed, Ireland had less and less food and money. Landlords went bankrupt as their tenants failed to pay rents, and property taxes went up, ironically, to provide money to feed the starving. In an effort to lower their property values and thus their taxes, some of them evicted the peasants still living on their land and tore down their huts. Britain sent more and more soldiers to Ireland to enforce evictions and see that taxes were collected. This combination of military might and no food made the Irish even more resentful of the occupying British government. Though there was more food available now, no one had the money to buy it.

Matters were made even worse by a financial crisis in Britain in 1847. Wheat prices plummeted, railroad stocks fell, and many businesses went bankrupt. The British had less money to help the Irish, even if they had wanted to.

The winter of 1848 to 1849 was a nightmare for the Irish. They had gambled on the potato crop, spending every cent they had to buy seed potatoes that they planted in the spring; after all, the blight hadn't attacked the 1847 crop, so they had reason to hope that it was gone. But they were terribly wrong; the blight was still around and it devastated potatoes all over the island. Landlords kept evicting peasants, and the

British government kept raising Ireland's taxes in the vain hope that this would help the island pull itself up by its bootstraps. The poorest people shrank down to human skeletons before dying. Some turned to crime as an alternative to starvation—in prison or on a ship heading to Australia there would at least be something to eat. Wealthier people gave up on Ireland and left for other countries.

## 72 } Results of the Famine

Ireland was a different place after the famine. The population was drastically reduced—an island of 8.2 million people in 1841 was reduced to 6 million in 1851. At least 1 million of those people had died. The rest fled the country, hoping for a new life in another land.

After the famine, there were fewer tiny landholdings, farms of 5 or fewer acres. By 1851, many more farms consisted of 30 acres or more. Fathers stopped dividing their acreage among all their sons and instead passed the entire farm to just one of them. This made it easier for a farmer to support his own family but caused problems for the children who didn't inherit. It also forced inheriting sons to wait longer to come into property, which delayed marriages. Farmers used more of their land to grow livestock; not surprisingly, they didn't grow nearly as many potatoes as they had before.

Many Irish left their beloved homeland during the famine years, hoping to find something better in the United States, England, Canada, or Australia. Emigration posed its own risks. Many emigrants died en route to their destinations. Others found that their new homes were little better than the barren farms they'd left behind. Nevertheless, many Irish emigrants quickly grew roots in fresh soil and flourished. For better or for worse, the Irish were now permanently planted around the world.

Daniel O'Connell had worked hard on behalf of the starving Irishmen, petitioning Parliament to put a stop to grain exports and to provide public work for people in need. He continued his support of nonviolent means of dealing with the Crown, but at the same time, a group called Young Ireland appeared. This was a group of younger men who were more interested in gaining Irish independence than in improving the existing system. After O'Connell died in 1847, the Young Irelanders were ready to use violence to fight for an Irish republic.

The Young Irelanders tried to foment a rebellion in 1848. They weren't prepared for it, and it fizzled quickly. Some of their leaders were captured and transported to Australia; others fled to the United States. Prominent among them were William Smith O'Brien, Thomas Francis Meagher (MAH-her), John Mitchel, and John Boyle O'Reilly. These men and others like them were responsible for spreading word throughout the world of Britain's handling of the famine. They also became prominent citizens of the New World and Ireland; for example, Meagher fought as a general for the Union Army in the American Civil War and went on to become governor of Montana. Mitchel later returned to Ireland and became mayor of Tipperary.

The famine did a lot to foster a feeling of unity among the Irish against the English. Dedication to the Catholic Church increased and priests grew more powerful. The Irish especially hated the landlord-tenant system, which had forced so many of them out of their homes. People across the country formed societies to protect tenants by fixing rents and getting farmers to promise not to take over the lands of evicted tenants. Irish politicians began pushing the tenant agenda in Parliament, and their efforts formed the start of Ireland's independence movement.

On St. Patrick's Day 1858 a former Young Ireland leader named James Stephens founded the Irish Republican Brotherhood. Around the same time, another rebel named Jeremiah O'Donovan Rossa founded a similar Phoenix Society in Skibbereen. These movements spread rapidly during the late 1850s. Though they were strongly condemned by the Catholic Church, these independence movements continued to gather steam and plan insurrections that would lead to an Irish republic.

The great famine has inspired more than its fair share of historical interpretations, many of which are wildly contradictory. The Irish used to say, "God gave us the potato blight, but the English gave us the famine." There is some truth to this statement, but it's not entirely fair to the English. They didn't understand the scope of the problem, and some of their policies made matters worse, but the fact remains that many people would have starved even with better help.

# PART 4

# Emigration to Modern Life

Irish demographics reveal two startling facts: There are around 70 million people worldwide who claim Irish descent, and Ireland today has barely half the population that it had 160 years ago, a decline unmatched in the modern world. These facts are explained and connected by the undeniable social reality of nineteenth-century Ireland—emigration.

## 73 } Why The Irish Left—and Where They Went

No one kept careful track of how many people left Ireland in the nineteenth century, but it certainly was a large number. People started leaving long before the Great Famine began in 1845; in the thirty years that preceded it, at least 1 million people left Ireland. Between the start of the famine and 1870, another 3 million or so emigrated. A decreased population and a lower birthrate decreased the flow of emigrants in the following years, but a significant proportion of the population continued to leave well into the twentieth century.

The two overpowering causes for emigration were hunger and poverty. The Great Famine and the half-dozen other potato failures of the nineteenth century sent millions of Irish people overseas. People saw the death and suffering around them; rather than wait for death in a land with no food, they picked up everything and sailed across the Atlantic.

But long before the famine struck and years after its end, young Irish people were leaving their homeland. The basic economic facts of Ireland were not promising: the island was small, with few natural resources beyond farmland; most of the best land was tied up in the hands of the Anglo-Irish aristocracy, and the rest was split up among more people than it could support; and English policies inhibited the development of Irish industries, which might have provided a way off the farms. Young Irish men and women realized that if they wanted any hope of a better life, they had to go overseas. If families were lucky enough to own land, younger sons often emigrated in order to clear the way to inheritance for the oldest.

Some young people left Ireland as seasonal migrants. Instead of setting up a new home in the New World, they would travel to another country for seasonal work, in agriculture or the fisheries, and then return home when the work was done for the year. The sons of small farmers were especially likely to do this; their periodic wages helped the family hold on to its property.

There were also non-economic reasons to leave Ireland. Some people, particularly a number of Nationalist revolutionaries, emigrated to avoid legal trouble and to drum up support for their cause in the New World. Others left to join family and friends overseas.

Where people went changed over time. During the nineteenth century, the vast majority of Irish emigrants went to the United States. Many also went to Canada, with a substantial proportion of those winding up in the United States after a few years. England and Scotland were always viable options, because the trip over was less expensive and less permanent. More distant English colonies, like Australia and South Africa, also saw a good number of Irish immigrants, although many of the newcomers to Australia weren't there of their own free will—the English sent prisoners and rebels to Australia.

Where people were from in Ireland played a part in where they wound up. Most of the people from the southwest and west ended up in the United States, while families from the north more commonly went to Canada. A long-standing tradition of migrant laborers going seasonally from Donegal to Scotland made Scotland the favored destination for Ireland's northwest. People in the east were more likely to head over to England.

The number of emigrants dropped significantly in the twentieth century. A trend of anti-immigrant sentiment swept the United States, making it less popular as a destination. From the 1930s on, an increasing percentage of Irish immigrants moved to British cities such as Liverpool, London, and Edinburgh. These cities offered the job prospects of an industrialized society, but they were close enough to home that people could make the trip back for the holidays. Large Irish communities developed in these cities, offering emigrants cultural continuity, a chance to practice their religion, and a degree of political influence.

## 74 } The Hardships of Emigration

Choosing to emigrate was not an easy decision. In a culture in which family and community ties were so strong, the decision to leave it all behind was heart-wrenching. Emigrants knew that they would probably never see their loved ones again. Friends and family often held mock wakes for emigrants on the night before their departure, symbolic of the permanent separation that was coming between them.

The price of the passage was the first difficulty most emigrants faced. Tickets for the overpacked transport ships weren't very expensive, but the people who wanted to leave were usually poor. Sometimes landlords and government programs assisted poor people with the price of a ticket.

The voyage overseas could be perilous, and it became especially dangerous during the famine years. The ships carrying emigrants during the famine became known as "coffin ships." The death rates onboard these ships were appallingly high; for example, one-fifth of the people who traveled from Cork to Quebec died in the process.

The owners of ships that specialized in transporting poor passengers fleeing the famine did not pay much attention to shipboard conditions. Dozens or hundreds of emigrants were packed into cargo holds with poor ventilation, little light, and rudimentary sanitation at best. Food was generally inadequate—think rancid meat and flour full of weevils. Under these conditions, diseases such as typhus and cholera ran rampant. Their immune systems already weakened by hunger, poor emigrants fell easy prey to the pathogens that lurked in the murky cargo holds.

Reaching port was just a first step; many Irish died after arriving in the New World but before they could legally set foot on the mainland. Canada was closer to Ireland than the United States, and many ships docked there. It was easier for ships to land in Canada for another reason—the United States put far more restrictions on emigrant ships, particularly in the matter of health. A ship full of feverish passengers couldn't land in the United States, which didn't want to take care of ailing paupers.

Many ships traveled up the St. Lawrence River to the quarantine island of Grosse Île, near Quebec City. In the summer of 1847, thousands of Irish immigrants crowded into the small hospital there; many of them died quickly, which freed up beds for the next round of sick people. Bodies were stacked high in the hot summer sun. Towns on the river would try to send boats to the next place upstream; no one wanted to keep these crowds of sick Irish.

Surviving the voyage and the quarantine didn't guarantee further survival. Immigrants who wanted to continue to Boston, New York, or other U.S. destinations would sometimes walk across the border from Montreal. This finished off many more people, especially those faced with a Canadian winter.

## 75 } The Immigrant Experience in the United States

For centuries, the United States has loomed in the Irish consciousness as the place to go for a new life. The United States offered the things that the Irish could not find at home: land, economic opportunities, and freedom from English control. With land resources vastly greater than those of Ireland, the United States seemed like a place of limitless possibilities. For people who chafed under British rule, the United States stood out as the colony that had made itself free.

After Cromwell sacked Ireland in the mid-seventeenth century, he sent Irish prisoners over to the West Indies as slave labor. Many of these forced immigrants eventually made their way to the English colonies in the New World; the Catholic colony of Maryland was a popular destination.

Irish immigrants had arrived in America in a steady stream throughout the eighteenth century. Most of the first voluntary Irish immigrants came from Ulster in the north of Ireland. These immigrants were generally, although not exclusively, Protestants. They were known as "Scotch-Irish" or "Scots Irish," because of the large number of Scots who settled in Ulster during the plantations of the seventeenth century. They quickly became an established component of U.S. society. Several U.S. presidents, including Andrew Jackson, James Polk, and Woodrow Wilson, were of Scotch-Irish descent.

In the nineteenth century, when a rapidly expanding population combined with a series of potato failures, millions of Irish decided to make the trip to the New World. Although the Scotch-Irish immigrants continued to arrive, the vast majority of the new arrivals were Catholics from the south of Ireland. Irish immigrants began to arrive in the United States' eastern cities in large numbers in the 1820s and then flooded in during the years of the famine. They headed for the big cities—New York, Philadelphia, Boston, Baltimore, and Chicago—and they usually stayed there.

These new immigrants tended to have a tougher time of it than their Protestant predecessors, and they faced a great deal of anti-Irish prejudice from the people already living in the United States. This was for a number of reasons: they came in far larger numbers; they were mostly poor farmers and unskilled laborers; they came at a time when most land in the East was already settled; and they were Catholics moving into a mostly Protestant land. Immigrants who deluged U.S. cities in the late 1840s were especially unwelcome because of their extreme poverty and frequently poor health.

The massive influx of newcomers caused a strain with the existing populations. In the years when the majority of the Irish arrived, U.S. cities had not yet figured out how they would handle immigrants. Consequently, the immigrants wound up figuring it out for themselves.

Most of the immigrants were uneducated and unskilled, so at first they could only take on menial tasks. But hard work in the United States was better than starving to death back in Ireland, so the Irish immigrants quickly developed a reputation as hard workers. The great wave of Irish immigration happened at a time of tremendous growth in U.S. cities and industries. Factories, apartment buildings, bridges, and railroads all needed to be built, and Irish immigrants were there to build them. In 1847, a New York newspaper wrote, "There are several sorts of power working at the fabric of this Republic: waterpower, steampower, horsepower, and Irish power."

Because so many Irish-Americans were in the building trades, they quickly took hold of a tool that was still rare back in Ireland—labor unions. The strong Irish sense of community allowed them to quickly grasp the strength of unity and collective bargaining. Irishmen soon led unions for bricklayers, carpenters, and plumbers. Many Irish families are still active leaders in the labor movement.

Irish immigrants arrived in cities that often did not want them and did not have an infrastructure in place to take care of them. To address these problems, immigrants fell back on the tribal cohesiveness that had governed their rural communities in Ireland. While the Irish newcomers did not have status, they did have numbers. This allowed them to focus their power on a political level, almost exclusively through the Democratic Party. The resulting political organizations were the first of America's political "machines"—organizations that used tight community organization to take power over local government, and then used government patronage to maintain their power.

The Tammany machine in New York was the prototype for this style of politics. Bosses Tweed and Croker oversaw tightly controlled political organizations that offered favors—food, clothing, social services—in exchange for votes. Once in power, they exchanged jobs for kickbacks. The patronage jobs were largely in law enforcement and construction, which contributed to Irish dominance in the building trades. It was during this period that the stereotype of the Irish police officer became popular. The machine organizations were undeniably corrupt, but they did provide services to immigrant communities that they would not have had otherwise.

While some immigrants responded to their tough conditions by becoming cops, others chose an alternate path. The Irish mob sought to make money from the chaos of the United States' fast-growing cities. The Irish relied on old traditions of family and community loyalty, as well as a tradition of rural terrorism. Irish mobsters organized gambling, prostitution, and protection rackets in urban immigrant communities.

The Irish mob families never achieved great success, but they did manage to survive through the twentieth century. The Irish mob operated alongside the Mafia in several cities, notably Boston and Chicago. Many of them were active rumrunners during Prohibition.

The progressive gentrification of the Irish immigrant community, however, tended to undercut the appeal of crime. As more and more Irish families moved into the middle class, the gangsters lost the support networks and opportunities offered by an insular immigrant community. Once second- and third-generation Irish-Americans found that they could go to college and become professionals, the power of the mob began to die out.

Catholic Irish immigrants often met with hostility and contempt from the more established American populations. The Irish represented competition for jobs and political power. Also, as Catholics, they presented a challenge to a predominantly Protestant country. Many employers refused to hire the Irish, and some landlords wouldn't rent to them.

One area where the Irish clashed with established groups was the question of alcohol. The Puritan tradition in the United States generally frowned on alcohol, whereas Irish culture viewed it as a harmless indulgence. When the Temperance movement arose in the mid-nineteenth century, Irish saloons were some of its first targets. Political cartoons of the time depicted Irishmen as red-face buffoons, enslaved by the bottle.

Interestingly, some of the worst anti-Irish discrimination came from the Scotch-Irish, who wanted to make clear that they were a different group from the impoverished newcomers. They created social organizations that specifically excluded Irish Catholics, and they derided the social pretensions of the "lace curtain Irish"—Catholic immigrants who had managed to make it into the middle class.

Although the Irish had to overcome a great deal of social stigma, they eventually became a part of the American mainstream. This was partially due to the influx of more immigrants, but it was mostly due to economic advancement.

## 76 Irish Communities in Other Lands

As mentioned, Irish emigrants didn't restrict themselves to America. Many simply crossed the Irish channel to Great Britain. Others traveled to the opposite side of the globe to settle in Australia and New Zealand.

After the United States, England and Scotland were the top destinations for Irish emigrants. The trip was shorter and cheaper, so it was easier to get there and easier to get back. The Irish went there in great numbers to pursue jobs in the textile mills, coal mines, and other businesses of the burgeoning Industrial Revolution. They primarily went to the industrial cities, like London and Liverpool. The total Irish population in England—

including both immigrants and their children born in England—numbered as much as 1.5 million people by the late nineteenth century.

Like America, England offered jobs. Unlike America, however, it did not offer much social mobility. English society had strong class lines, and elements of old anti-Irish and anti-Catholic prejudices still operated. Irish immigrants usually lived in large city slums. They rarely exercised much political power, and they generally remained in low-level jobs. This situation did not begin to improve until the early twentieth century.

Irish people had been settling in Australia unintentionally for decades before large-scale emigration began—Australia was Great Britain's biggest prison, and many Irish were sentenced to life there. Their crimes often seem paltry compared to such a major punishment. For the offense of stealing clothes or threatening a landlord, an individual could be sentenced to exile on the other side of the Earth for the rest of his or her life—a sentence known as "transportation."

Relatively few Irish emigrated intentionally to Australia or New Zealand, largely because the long journey was four times more expensive than passage to the United States, but those who went found a vast and sparsely populated land. They encountered some of the old English prejudices, but in a land where most of the people had arrived as prisoners, being Irish or Catholic was not a serious impediment to social advancement. Many Irish immigrants soon became wealthy through farming and wool production.

This outflow of people had a tremendous impact, both on Ireland and on the destination countries. By 1890, some 3 million Irish-born people lived in other countries. In Ireland, it meant that the remaining population had a better chance of getting by, but it also meant a degree of stagnation. By taking away the youngest and most vigorous members of the workforce, emigration deprived Ireland of the surplus manpower that could have fueled an industrial revolution. Instead, Irish muscles powered the factories of England and the United States.

Another impact of losing the young population was that it made revolution in Ireland unlikely. With its youngsters gone, the remaining population tended toward conservatism. While Ireland in the late nineteenth century certainly had its share of revolutionaries, one has to wonder what would have happened if all the angry young men running the political machines in Boston and New York had stayed home. It is noteworthy that Ireland's final revolt against England happened during World War I, when ordinary emigration policies had been suspended.

The story of Irish emigration isn't over. You'll still frequently run into authentic Irish accents in the many pubs of Boston and New York. Thousands of young Irish men and women emigrate every year. The difference, however, is their reason for leaving. Today, Irish people emigrate for education, or for job relocations, or because they've always heard how much fun Boston is. The days of people leaving because of hunger and poverty are over.

## 77 } The Rebirth of Nationalism (Meanwhile, Back in Ireland . . . )

The Ireland that dragged itself out of the Great Hunger was changed forever. Lingering resentment began to take shape, leading to an organized political movement for independence. Eventually, the forces of Irish Nationalism won their independence but the violent path they chose has left scars to this day.

The Irish Nationalist movement rose out of the anger people felt about the famine and the continuing economic disparities of their island. It first manifested itself in agrarian secret societies—groups of farmers and laborers who secretly gathered in the countryside to enforce their own views of justice, usually against landowners and their agents. Groups like this had existed for over a century, but in the 1850s their campaigns of rural terrorism and economic sanctions became more aggressive and targeted specifically the English. The most powerful of these secret societies was the Irish Republican Brotherhood (IRB), known commonly as the Fenians.

The principal mover behind the Fenians was James Stephens, a fiery orator with a gift for organization and a vague notion of an independent Irish nation. John O'Mahoney, the head of the powerful U.S. Fenian chapter, was his ally. Stephens and O'Mahoney built the Fenian Brother-hood into a secret, semi-revolutionary society with thousands of members. They founded the newspaper *Irish People* to express their desire for land reform and Irish independence.

Fenians in Ireland were mostly Catholic farmers and shopkeepers who had little political power. So the Fenian leaders decided that their greatest chance for success lay not in politics but in armed revolt, just like Wolfe Tone had envisioned in 1798. Working with O'Mahoney, Stephens actively recruited Irish-American Civil War veterans to come fight for Ireland.

In 1867 the Fenians took action. They didn't have enough weapons to pose any real threat to British military power, but they hoped that an act of armed defiance would encourage the people to rise up against England. They launched several raids to steal weapons from police and coastguard stations; unfortunately for them, the people did not rally to their aid as they had hoped, and most of their fighters got caught. The English quickly broke up the Fenian military organization and imprisoned its leaders. They executed Fenian leaders William Allen, Michael Larkin, and Michael O'Brien on dubious legal grounds. These men became known as the Manchester Martyrs.

## 78 } The Home Rule Party

The Fenians kept (quietly) calling for armed revolt. But in the following decades the banner of Irish Nationalism moved away from the rifle and into the realm of politics.

After the famine, both Catholics and Protestants had begun to feel that the English could not rule their island effectively and justly. Although they had their own differences, an uneasy coalition of conservative Protestants and liberal Catholics got together and formed the Home Rule Party. This party got a bunch of its members into Parliament at the same time that a liberal, Prime Minister William Gladstone, was emerging as a giant in British politics.

Gladstone realized that Ireland's complaints against England were justified and that England's presence in Ireland was based on a tradition of injustice; at the same time, he felt that the Home Rulers were too radical. He tried to defuse the Home Rule movement by enacting landmark legislation to address Irish grievances—killing home rule with kindness. His first act, in 1868, declared that the Protestant Church of Ireland was no longer the official religion of the entire country. Most Irish loved this. The act was cheered in Dublin but condemned in Belfast, where the population was mostly Protestant.

Gladstone's most important reforms were his Land Acts of 1870 and 1881. Before these acts, the average Irish farmer rented his farmland (usually from an English landowner) and lived in constant fear of eviction. The Land Acts granted these farmers protection against unreasonable rents and unfair evictions, and made it easier for them to buy land. Over time, the Land Acts greatly improved the lives of many farmers, and Gladstone's strategy might well have defused the Home Rule movement, if not for the emergence of one of Ireland's most charismatic leaders—Charles Stewart Parnell.

Parnell was handsome, impassioned, and articulate, and he took Parliament by storm. People didn't know what to make of him; he was a wealthy Protestant landowner, but at the same time he supported the radical Nationalist politics of poor Catholic farmers. He entered Parliament in 1875 as the representative for County Meath. His confident oratory and uncompromising dedication to land reform instantly made him a leader of the Home Rule Party. When he felt that Irish issues were being ignored in Parliament, he recruited his fellow Irish MPs to obstruct parliamentary proceedings until his issues were heard.

Parnell was president of the Land League, a farmers' organization that called for relief of exorbitant rents, more lenient eviction policies, and easier land ownership for small farmers. Gladstone's Land Acts had made some progress on these fronts, but that progress was too slow for Parnell. His Land League insisted that farmers evicted from their property should hold their ground, and it tacitly condoned the use of boycotts and violence against landlords who took possession of an evicted tenant's land. This period of rural intimidation and economic sanction became known as the Land War.

Gladstone didn't approve of Parnell's obstructionist policies and endorsement of Land League violence; he had Parnell arrested and thrown in Kilmainham Jail in 1881. Parnell continued to run his political machine from jail, and he achieved unprecedented popularity in Ireland for his defiance of the prime minister.

Both Parnell and Gladstone, however, realized that they needed to work together to achieve real reform. They carried on secret negotiations through two intermediaries, Captain Willie O'Shea and his wife, Katherine (Kitty). Gladstone and Parnell eventually reached a settlement called the Kilmainham Treaty, in which Parnell restrained Land League violence in exchange for his release and Gladstone's cooperation on a more powerful Land Act.

In the 1885 election, Parnell's Home Rulers took 85 of the 103 Irish seats in Parliament. It appeared that some form of constitutional solution to home rule was in sight. In 1886 Parnell and Gladstone brought forth a Home Rule Bill to finally give Ireland a form of independence.

There was a big problem, though—the Protestants in the northern part of Ireland (Ulster) didn't want home rule. The rise of the Home Rule Party called attention for the first time to a phenomenon that Irish Nationalists had traditionally ignored and would continue to ignore to their detriment—the loyalty of Ulster Unionists (those who wanted Ireland to remain part of the United Kingdom). That's why Protestants had founded the Orange Order during the time of Wolfe Tone. That's also why they created the militant Ulster Defence Association after Gladstone disestablished the Protestant Church in Ireland in 1868.

The 1886 Home Rule Bill didn't pass; it had too much opposition from Ulster and the British House of Lords, who still liked the idea of Ireland as part of the British Empire. Parnell regathered his forces and prepared to try again, but personal affairs suddenly intruded—Willie O'Shea divorced his wife, Kitty, and named Parnell as her lover. It was a huge scandal. Remember, the O'Sheas had served as Parnell's intermediaries for the

Kilmainham Treaty. The trial revealed that Parnell and Kitty had been carrying on a passionate affair since then. Captain O'Shea had known about the affair for years; Kitty had already had three children with Parnell.

The case shocked both liberal Englishmen and Catholic Irishmen. Gladstone ended his alliance with Parnell, fearing that his own party in England wouldn't support him if he stuck with the Irishman. Parnell fell from power.

Parnell didn't give up. He married Kitty O'Shea and began a fierce campaign to retake his position in the party. His charisma and political skill were such that he might have actually succeeded, but a fever killed him suddenly in 1891. Kitty was beside him when he died. With Parnell's death, the Home Rule movement lost its momentum, and it didn't truly regain it for another twenty-five years.

# 79⟩ A Celtic Revival

The Home Rule Party continued to press for a parliamentary solution, but without Parnell, it lacked the organization to push it through. The remaining members kept fighting with one another, which diffused their political power. Gladstone sponsored a second Home Rule Bill in 1893, but the same opposition from Conservatives and Ulster Unionists killed it. Ironically, the success of the very Land Acts and other liberal measures that the Home Rule Party had pushed for had taken the wind out of its sails. The state of civil rights and living conditions for the Irish people had significantly improved in recent years, so the need for home rule seemed less intense.

While political efforts at nationalism were stuck in a rut, arts and culture saw a huge surge of interest in all things Irish. The English traditionally thought of the Irish as uncouth barbarians, but a new generation of the Irish looked into their island's past and proved the English wrong.

Intellectuals like William Butler Yeats, Douglas Hyde, and Lady Augusta Gregory called for the preservation and appreciation of Irish storytelling, Celtic art, and the fast-fading Irish language. Hyde founded the Gaelic League to promote the Irish language. By 1906 there were more than 900 branches, with more than 100,000 members. In 1903 Yeats and Gregory founded the Irish National Theatre at the Abbey Theatre in Dublin and promoted the production of distinctively Irish plays.

Athletics were another focus of nationalist energy. The Gaelic Athletic Association, founded in 1884, promoted the distinctively Irish sports of Gaelic football and hurling.

In these expressions of Irish culture, many Irish people realized for the first time that they had a history and culture every bit as worthy as the English. While these movements had little direct political impact, they provided Irish people with an identity and a rallying point for their nationalist feelings.

Although the independence movement had entered a period of contented inaction, radical Nationalism hadn't disappeared. The IRB (the group that organized the Fenian uprising) was still around, but its call for armed revolt seemed more and more like the talk of cranky old men.

The movement for an independent republic took a quiet step forward in 1905 when a publisher named Arthur Griffith founded a new political party called Sinn Féin, Irish for "ourselves alone." Griffith promoted the Nationalist cause in a newspaper called the *United Irishman*, after Wolfe Tone's old organization. Sinn Féin was a relatively small party throughout the prewar years, but it provided radicals and intellectuals with a place to discuss aggressive alternatives to the slow constitutional path to home rule.

# 80} An Ireland Divided

Home rule made no progress in the Conservative-controlled Parliament of the first decade of the twentieth century. But when the Liberals swept back into power in 1910 behind Prime Minister Herbert Henry Asquith, Ireland was at the top of their agenda. In 1912, Asquith brought forward the third Home Rule Bill, which reached further than any of its predecessors and enjoyed wide popularity among the Irish people.

There was one section of the Irish population, however, that still opposed home rule—the Ulster Protestants. Seeing the latest Home Rule Bill as the final step toward separation, the members of the Orange Order rose up against it. They organized the Ulster Volunteer Force (UVF), a paramilitary group committed to defending Ulster's union with England.

The UVF began drilling and stockpiling weapons. By 1914 there were estimated to be more than 100,000 men ready to fight for the UVF.

In response, Nationalists in the south began their own paramilitary organization called the Irish Volunteers. The Volunteers was initially organized by the remnants of the IRB, although its politics was generally closer to the moderates of the Home Rule Party. The Volunteers claimed to have more than 100,000 members as well, though it had fewer weapons than its rivals in the North.

The Ulster dilemma froze the Home Rule Bill in its tracks. Although the Liberals may have had sufficient votes to push the bill through, it was politically very awkward to push away a big group of loyal British subjects, especially when those subjects were threatening to fight to stay in. A favored solution to this problem was to grant home rule and then use the British army to enforce it in Ulster. This proposal faltered when the mutiny at the Curragh revealed that British army officers were opposed to fighting Ulster troops.

The second set of options revolved around some form of partition, in effect dividing Ireland into two states. There were nine counties in the traditional province of Ulster, but only six of them had large Protestant populations, and in 1910 only four of them had Protestant majorities. Unionists and Nationalists suggested different partition plans. Some supported having all of Ulster split off and stay with the United Kingdom, which might have facilitated reunification in the future. Others thought it would be better if only those counties with Protestant majorities broke away from the Irish nation. Both sides spent the next four years wrangling

over various proposals, but none met the approval of both the Unionist
and the Nationalist sides.

# 81 } World War I and The Easter Rebellion

In August 1914, outside events suddenly changed the whole debate. World
War I was breaking out in Europe, and Parliament wanted to solve the
Irish problem quickly so that it could concentrate on the coming war. John
Redmond, the leader of the Home Rulers, offered the United Kingdom
the use of the Irish Volunteers for home defense in exchange for a provisional acceptance of the Home Rule Bill, leaving aside the Ulster question
for the time being. Asquith's Parliament agreed, and the bill was put on
the books with the proviso that it would not go into effect until a year had
passed or the war was over. Both sides saw this as a way to move forward
on the Ireland issue without coming to a final decision on Ulster.

The act was immediately received as a tremendous step forward for
Ireland, and Nationalists felt free for the first time in decades to express
British patriotism. Thousands of young men from all parts of Ireland
came forward to serve in the war, including many members of the UVF
and the Irish Volunteers. In the early days, morale was high.

As the war ground on, however, Irish opinions began to turn. Not only
did the war delay the enactment of home rule, but each month brought
new lists of Irish casualties from the battlefields of Europe as well. The

British military didn't accept Redmond's offer to use the Volunteers, nor did it arm them for home defense. It was rumored that the English draft would soon spread to Ireland. To make matters worse, a change in government put Ulster Unionist leaders in the British Cabinet, making Nationalists suspect that home rule might be delayed indefinitely. It was in this environment that the radicals in the IRB and Sinn Féin decided to make their move.

On April 24, 1916, Easter Monday, a group of armed Irish Volunteers moved into the General Post Office in Dublin and occupied the building. Patrick Pearse (or Pádraig MacPiarais), a schoolteacher and Sinn Féin activist, read the Proclamation of the Irish Republic, a statement declaring Ireland's independence. Simultaneously, armed Volunteers took over other significant buildings throughout the city.

The uprising was a surprise for Unionists and Nationalists alike; with home rule already on the books, armed revolution seemed a little extreme. British troops were quickly sent into the city, and soon much of central Dublin was in flames. The Volunteers lacked either the arms or the organization to put up a real military resistance to the British army, and after a week the last of the rebels surrendered. The fighting killed 450, and afterward more than 1,000 Irish were sent to prisons in England.

At the time of the Easter Rebellion, most Irish people—even Nationalists—didn't think violence was the answer to Ireland's problems. Ensuing events, however, soon led to a change in opinions.

In May of 1916, the British army began executing leaders of the rebellion. They shot or hanged sixteen men. Most Irish thought that they had decided to execute the prisoners much too hastily and without fair trials. In addition, there were reports of bad treatment of imprisoned rebels. The British released the remaining prisoners by Christmas 1916, primarily as a gesture to help bring the United States into the war, but that did little to quiet emotions in Ireland.

## 82 } War of Independence

Prime Minister Asquith appointed David Lloyd George (who would replace Asquith as prime minister later that year) to resolve the Irish home rule question once and for all. Lloyd George, relying heavily on the advice of Unionist associates, settled on a compromise in which Ireland got home rule but the six majority Protestant counties in the north remained part of the Union (the British Empire).

To southern Nationalists, this was unacceptable. To make matters worse, the British army seized the weapons from Irish Volunteer groups in the south but allowed UVF forces to keep theirs. People in the south began to believe that the Home Rule Bill on the books was a charade.

This gave Sinn Féin its big chance. Led by Éamon de Valera, a half-American mathematician who had taken part in the Easter Rebellion, Sinn Féin began to take Parliament seats away from the traditional home rule candidates. Sinn Féin's stated goal was an independent, unified Republic of Ireland.

Sinn Féin's parliamentary successes were limited to Nationalist hotbeds until the British government gave them two great boosts: first, it extended army conscription to Ireland, an act the Irish had dreaded for years; second, it arrested de Valera and other Sinn Féin leaders on vague and insubstantial charges of a plot against the government. Both actions were highly unpopular, and they convinced the majority of the Irish that the British government was not serious about letting Ireland run its own affairs.

While Sinn Féin was taking the road of politics, a twenty-seven-year-old Easter Rebellion veteran named Michael Collins was exploring an alternate path. Working with the IRB and the Irish Volunteers, he began organizing a paramilitary force that could put guns behind Sinn Féin's claims of independence. This force became known as the Irish Republican Army—the IRA.

Most Irish people deplored the IRA killings. Collins calculated that his systematic terrorism would provoke the English into an overly aggressive response. And that's exactly what happened.

The British shipped thousands of soldiers to Ireland and created a new police force called the Black and Tans to help keep the peace. The Black and Tans were composed primarily of former British soldiers who had neither the police training nor the familiarity with Ireland that the sensitive situation demanded. These men found Ireland very stressful— the people who murdered their fellow officers were indistinguishable from the people they were supposed to protect. So they responded with a campaign of reprisals that matched the IRA's in brutality.

This period of guerilla strikes and police reprisals is known as the Anglo-Irish War. Both sides lost hundreds of men. The IRA made little military headway, but the war's impact on the opinions of the Irish people was devastating to the British. The peacekeeping strategy backfired—the brutal and often indiscriminate reprisals of the Black and Tans convinced people that Sinn Féin was right after all and that Great Britain was a repressive occupier that would only relinquish Ireland if forced out.

The conflict was simultaneously playing havoc with British politics. English civilians were shocked by the daily stories of police brutality in Ireland. In composing the Treaty of Versailles at the end of the war, Britain claimed that World War I had been fought to protect the rights of small countries to determine their own fates, and yet it had a small country in its own backyard demanding its own rights.

Prime Minister Lloyd George called for a cease-fire and treaty negotiations. The fact that he was offering a treaty was significant; only sovereign nations can sign treaties with one another, so his offer made clear that independence was on the table. The Sinn Féin and IRA leaders agreed to the cease-fire, and a group of ambassadors led by Arthur Griffith and Michael Collins went to London in 1921 to negotiate.

Both sides agreed that Ireland would take a dominion status similar to that enjoyed by Canada—independent, but still a part of the British Empire. The chief sticking points were whether the Irish would have to swear an oath to the king, and the final settlement of the Ulster question.

After skillful negotiating by a British team including Lloyd George and Winston Churchill, the Irish contingent largely gave in on both points. The final Treaty of Peace between Great Britain and Ireland did not demand that Irish citizens swear allegiance to the king, but it did require them to recognize his dominion over Ireland. More significantly, the treaty established the six-county partition of Ulster pushed for by Unionists since 1914. This action, called Partition, created the political entity called Northern Ireland.

Collins signed the treaty, saying it was the best that Ireland could achieve under the current conditions. After a bitter struggle, it was passed by the Dáil (the new Irish Parliament). Not everyone was happy, however; Éamon de Valera condemned the treaty, as did the majority of radical Nationalists in the IRA. These Nationalists said that they had fought for a united Ireland, and they wouldn't take one cut into pieces. And so the Irish Civil War (1921–23) began.

# 83 } Irish Civil War

Like all civil wars, this one was marked by bitterness and atrocity. Collins was forced to organize an official military response against the same IRA men he had fought beside for years. Hundreds died, and Collins himself

was killed in an ambush. The anti-treaty forces, however, did not have the
support of the populace, and it was soon clear that they could not win.
To stop the bloodshed, Éamon de Valera announced that it was time for
Ireland to accept the treaty and move on.

Ireland had peace and independence at last, but not without a cost.
The scars of the Civil War haunted Irish politics for decades. More significantly, the division between the Irish Free State in the South and
Northern Ireland had become real and immovable. Unionists in Northern Ireland, appalled by the violence of the Anglo-Irish and Civil Wars,
resolved more strongly than ever to remain part of the United Kingdom.
This unnatural division between North and South has plagued people on
both sides of the border to this day.

When the Irish Civil War ended, Ireland had peace and independence
at last. Over the next fifty years, the people of Ireland worked through the
difficult questions regarding their relationship with the United Kingdom,
the role of the Catholic Church in their government, and the thorny question of Northern Ireland

## 84 } Irish Free State

The Ireland that emerged from the Anglo-Irish Treaty in 1921 was known
as the Irish Free State. In many ways, it had the independence that Irish
Nationalists had dreamed about for years. It had its own Parliament, the Dáil

Éireann (doyl ay-ran), which was responsible for Ireland's social and economic affairs. It inherited a British government infrastructure that allowed it to jump quickly into efficient self-government. Police and Irish home defense forces were now entirely under Ireland's control, with a new, unarmed police force known as the Garda Síochána (GAR-dah sho-HA-na).

But the Free State still maintained a number of ties to England. It was still subject to British international policy, a point made clear by the naval bases that the British navy maintained at Irish ports. A British "governor" continued to serve in Dublin, although the role was largely symbolic. The most powerful symbolic gesture was that Irish civil servants were required to swear the Oath of Fidelity (also known as the Oath of Allegiance) to the British Empire before they could serve. These remnants of the old relationship with England played a powerful role in the course of Irish Free State politics.

The civil-war beginning of the Irish Free State accounts for the curious political divisions of twentieth-century Ireland: the fundamental political divisions in Ireland developed around those who supported the Anglo-Irish Treaty and those who opposed it, rather than on the Liberal/Conservative or Labor/Business lines seen in the political systems of most modern democratic states.

The victorious pro-treaty faction created a political party called Cumann na nGaedheal (ku-man na gah-yehl), which had been the original name of Sinn Féin in 1900. Cumann na nGaedheal formed the basis of the Free State government. Its leader, William T. Cosgrave, tried to establish a stable Irish state within its constitutional boundaries as a British dominion.

But the opponents of the Anglo-Irish Treaty were still an important force. The opposing party, Fianna Fáil (fee-AH-na foil), was created in 1926 by Éamon de Valera. Fianna Fáil maintained that the provisions of the Anglo-Irish Treaty—the Oath of Fidelity and the partition of Northern Ireland—were unacceptable compromises. Although de Valera had called a halt to military opposition to the treaty, he still believed that Ireland needed to assert its independence. Fianna Fáil had limited influence in the early days because its members refused to swear the Oath of Fidelity and thus could not take their seats in the Dáil.

The priority of the Free State government under Cumann na nGaedheal was to create a stable government. In 1924 a contingent of old IRA men within the Free State Army voiced objections to the new government. Rather than risk a military coup, the Free State government immediately removed all objectionable officers from power and placed the army under the command of a loyal Garda commander. The Irish Free State was going to be ruled by civil rather than military powers.

Éamon de Valera dominated twentieth-century Irish politics. He led Sinn Féin (1917–26), the Irish provisional government (1919–22), the anti-treaty forces (1922–25), and then Fianna Fáil (for the next fifty years). He served for sixteen years as *taoiseach* (prime minister) and nineteen years as president. He retired from politics at the age of ninety-one and died two years later, in 1975. Throughout, de Valera was known as a fervent patriot, a devout Catholic, and an incorruptible servant of his people.

## 85 } De Valera and The Fianna Fáil Path

De Valera was born in New York in 1882 to an Irish mother and a Spanish father—hence his unusual name. This made him an American, which he used to his advantage throughout his political career. When he was three, his father died and his mother sent him to Ireland to be raised by his grandmother in Bruree, County Limerick. He studied mathematics in Dublin and became a teacher. He also came to love the Irish language and became involved with the Gaelic League, which led to his extreme Nationalism.

De Valera was an intellectual and he looked the part—tall, thin, and bespectacled. He didn't stand out from the crowd until he ended up in prison after the Easter Rebellion; subsequently, his eloquent letters and well-thought-out arguments for Irish independence began to inspire a generation of young men, and they soon chose him as their leader.

In 1927 Fianna Fáil politicians agreed to take the Oath of Fidelity after an IRA assassination of a top Free State administrator threatened to renew factional violence. De Valera decided that the time had come to work within the constitutional framework in order to achieve his party's goals. This strategy became increasingly effective after the British Parliament passed the Statute of Westminster, which gave imperial dominions—Canada, India,

South Africa, and the Irish Free State—the right to disregard parliamentary actions that they did not believe should apply to them. Pushed to its logical conclusion, the Statute of Westminster effectively allowed dominions to make themselves independent in all but name.

This was the chance de Valera had been waiting for.

The 1932 general elections returned a majority of Fianna Fáil delegates to the Dáil. A few months afterward, de Valera announced that Ireland would no longer pay land annuities to England. These annuities were part of the Anglo-Irish Treaty: farmers who had benefited from English government loans to buy land were supposed to repay the loans to the Free State government, who would then hand the money over to England. But de Valera maintained that the land had been stolen from the Irish in the first place, so Ireland had a moral justification for withholding the annuity payments.

The act was popular in Ireland, but the British Treasury was not amused. It immediately began a system of retaliatory trade measures to punish Ireland. British tariffs increased the cost of Irish cattle imports by up to 80 percent. British markets constituted 96 percent of Irish exports at this time, so the tariffs were costly, although they were partially offset by not having to pay the land annuities. This period of trade retaliation was known unofficially as the Economic War.

Withholding the land annuities was a powerful statement of independence, but Fianna Fáil wanted to go further. In 1933 it passed legislation that removed the requirement for civil servants to swear the Oath of

Fidelity. Again, the British did not like to see another breach of the treaty, but the Statute of Westminster made the Irish action perfectly legal.

There were some in Ireland who thought that Fianna Fáil was going too far too fast. The old Free State politicians of Cumann na nGaedheal were still around, although their party had lost much of its power. In 1933, Cumann na nGaedheal joined with two smaller groups, the Centre Party and the National Guard, to form Fine Gael. The newly empowered Fine Gael advocated a more moderate position toward England than Fianna Fáil, and it tended to appeal more to large landholders and business interests, whereas Fianna Fáil traditionally appealed to small farmers and laborers. These differences aside, by European political standards the parties were, and still are, fairly close together ideologically. Fine Gael and Fianna Fáil have continued to this day as the two major parties of Irish politics.

Fianna Fáil took a further step in 1936 by removing references to the Crown and the British governor-general from the Irish Constitution. This was a direct challenge to the basis of the Anglo-Irish Treaty, but its reception in England was probably mitigated by the crisis over Edward VIII's abdication. In any event, it was clear that Ireland was in charge of its own constitution.

In 1937 de Valera made this point official by passing a new constitution that officially ended the Irish Free State of the Anglo-Irish Treaty. This new constitution established a number of key points: Ireland was now officially a nation called Éire; the nation of Éire consisted of the entire island of Ireland, including the six counties of the north; and it allowed for religious freedom but reserved a "special relationship" with the Catholic Church. The constitution also created the position of an Irish president. The first person to fill that role was Douglas Hyde, the scholar and patriot who forty years before had rallied nationalist feelings around the Gaelic League.

The reaction in England was resignation; the government under Prime Minister Arthur Neville Chamberlain was unwilling to fight the move, which was, after all, technically legal under the Statute of Westminster. The people in Northern Ireland were outraged by both the new constitution's claim to the entire island, and by the pro-Catholic position of the new country. If the two states had been far from reunification before, this step put them that much further apart. But by this time, de Valera and his Nationalist supporters had mostly given up hope of a near-term reunification of Ireland.

# 86 } World War II

The great test of Irish sovereignty came in 1939, when England and Germany went to war. The United Kingdom expected that Ireland would join the war against the Axis powers. Ireland refused. In addition, de Valera refused to allow the British navy to use its former naval bases on Irish soil. In Ireland, World War II was known as "the Emergency."

Ireland received a great deal of criticism for its choice of neutrality. Many English considered it a betrayal of their long-term relationship, and their government initiated an unofficial economic war of sanctions against Ireland. Americans were shocked that Ireland would not take an official stance against Germany. De Valera's government was under immense internal pressure as well, from a population whose sentiments were overwhelmingly on the side of the Allies.

But de Valera wanted to prove a point: Ireland was no longer a part of the British Empire, and the most decisive way to demonstrate that fact was to maintain firm neutrality in the war. One of the traditional arguments of the Republican movement had been that Irishmen should not have to die for another country's empire. It was a tough stance to take, but de Valera was not going to lose his chance to take it. Moreover, Ireland was in no condition to fight; years of warfare had reduced it to a state of poverty with an army of only 7,000 poorly equipped soldiers.

Despite the official stance of neutrality, Ireland did support the Allied cause in a number of quiet ways. Thousands of Irish citizens were allowed to volunteer for Allied armies. While downed German airmen were interned, downed Allied soldiers were promptly handed over to Northern Ireland. When Axis bombing set Belfast ablaze in 1941, de Valera promptly sent fire trucks from Dublin, Drogheda, and Dundalk to help combat the fire. Ireland also suffered its own war wounds: a German bombing raid intended for Liverpool lost its way and bombed Dublin, killing thirty-four civilians.

When the war was over, both British and American diplomats harbored resentment against Ireland's seemingly unfriendly stance. But to de Valera and his government, Ireland had demonstrated once and for all that it was in charge of its own destiny.

Meanwhile, Northern Ireland used the war to show its dedication to the United Kingdom. Thousands of Northern Ireland's citizens volunteered to fight. Belfast's shipbuilding industry played an important role in supplying warships for the British navy. Because of its economic importance to the Allied war effort, Belfast was the target of heavy German bombing; more than 1,200 people died in the "Belfast Blitz." Northern Ireland's sacrifices had a significant impact on its relationship with the British government in later years.

# 87} A New Republic

De Valera steered Ireland through the dangerous days of the Emergency, but he was not the one to cut Ireland's last ties to England. In 1948, after sixteen years of Fianna Fáil dominance, Fine Gael joined with the Labour Party and a radical Nationalist group called Clann na Poblachta (klan-na po-blah-ta) to create a coalition government.

It was a strange coalition: the moderates, leftists, and nationalists of the three parties could agree on little more than a common desire to unseat Fianna Fáil. The *taoiseach* in charge of this new government was John Costello, a Dublin lawyer who had served with Fine Gael for years.

In a meeting with the prime minister of Canada in 1948, Costello revealed that Ireland intended to declare itself a republic. The following year, with a unanimous vote of the Cabinet, Ireland officially removed itself from the British Commonwealth. Ireland was now officially the Republic of Ireland. It has continued in this form to the present day.

Parliament responded with the Ireland Act of 1949, which stated that Northern Ireland was still part of the United Kingdom and would remain so until the people of Northern Ireland consented to leave. This act directly contradicted the constitution of Ireland, which claimed Northern Ireland as part of the nation. In addition, the United Kingdom guaranteed to the people of Northern Ireland that their social security benefits would not be allowed to fall behind Britain's.

The effect of the Ireland Act was to seal the partition between Northern Ireland and the Republic more solidly than ever before. Politicians on both sides recognized this fact, and many criticized Costello's government for making an essentially symbolic gesture that ruined any chances of undoing Partition.

But what was done was done. The island of Ireland was now home to a British state and an independent republic, both looking anxiously across the border and wondering how they ended up so far apart.

By 1950, Ireland had finally resolved its long-standing questions about its government and its relationship with England. In the following years, the Irish government focused increasingly on economics. The country was still one of the poorest in Europe, and despite its political claims to independence, the Irish economy was heavily dependent on England for both import and export markets. These economic realities were underlined by Ireland's high rate of emigration. The Irish population had continued to drop in every census since the Great Famine of the 1840s.

Fianna Fáil regained power from Fine Gael in 1951 and held on to it for most of the next fifty years. Both parties, however, agreed on the basic solution to Ireland's economic problems: foreign investment, foreign loans, and a planned economy. The plan was to use foreign capital to build industries that would relieve Ireland's chronic unemployment.

The plans were successful. Ireland benefited from American Marshall Plan funds, and American and English businesses showed enthusiasm for investing in Ireland. The economy slowly developed, and by the 1960s the Irish standard of living was creeping toward the standard of Western Europe. The rate of emigration slowed down. The 1966 census showed, for the first time in more than 100 years, an increase in population.

Ireland eagerly took part in the developing multinational organizations of the postwar years. The Republic joined the UN in 1955 and the European Economic Community in 1972.

## 88 } Trouble in the North

While the Republic of Ireland worked out its path of independent development, Northern Ireland embraced its role as a loyal province of the United Kingdom. Northern Ireland's industries successfully pursued further economic ties with England, and the standard of living in the North continued to outpace that of the South.

Northern Ireland's image as a peaceful and prosperous British province, however, concealed a tension beneath the surface. There were still Irish Nationalists who wanted to undo Partition. Fianna Fáil maintained that Northern Ireland was part of Ireland, as shown by territorial claims in the 1937 constitution. The Protestant politicians of Northern Ireland staunchly denied these claims. In 1954 they passed the Flags and Emblems Act, which made it illegal to fly the tricolor Irish flag in Northern Ireland. Although politicians in the Republic often spoke of reuniting their country, the majority of them realized that, in practical terms, their claims were little more than rhetoric.

During the years when King Henry VIII and Queen Elizabeth I extended English control over most of Ireland, the northern counties of Ulster were regarded as the most "savage" part of the island. In the early 1600s, King James I decided to cure Ulster of its Catholicism by displacing the Irish and settling English and Scottish Protestants there. This settlement became known as the Ulster Plantation.

As a result, the northern and southern regions of the island developed along different lines. While the predominantly Catholic population in the rest of Ireland continued in the traditional Irish jobs of farming and animal husbandry, the largely Protestant population in Ulster embraced the industrial revolution. Belfast became a center of the shipbuilding and linen textile industries. By the nineteenth century, the average person in Ulster was considerably wealthier than his or her southern counterparts.

The prosperity of the north, however, was mostly prosperity for Protestants. The Scots and English who had settled there were keenly aware that their land had been seized from the Irish, and they never lost their anxiety that the previous inhabitants might try to take it back. As in the Protestant Ascendancy, they enforced a social and legal code designed to repress Catholics. Even after O'Connell's reforms had begun to liberate Ireland's Catholics, the people of Ulster dutifully maintained an unofficial system of repression.

Ulster Protestant anxieties rose as the Irish Nationalist movement grew. Unionists in the north blocked the passage of a series of home rule bills, and they formed a variety of organizations, such as the United Orangemen and the Ulster Volunteers. The havoc of the Anglo-Irish War and the Irish Civil War further polarized the Protestant stance.

Northern Ireland was created in 1921 as a semiautonomous state, still tied to the British Empire—this was part of the agreement that Michael Collins and other Irish Nationalists made with the British. Northern Ireland ruled itself through an independent administration at Stormont, outside Belfast. For nearly fifty years the region remained largely peaceful, but just beneath the orderly veneer the coals of deep-seated resentment smoldered.

Northern Ireland's approximately 550,000 Catholics never shared equally in the state's prosperity. They officially had all the rights guaranteed by the British Constitution, but unspoken rules kept them a distinct underclass—many companies wouldn't hire Catholics, and many landlords wouldn't rent to them. Most of them worked in low-paying, unskilled jobs. Although Catholics made up 31 percent of the labor force, they only accounted for 6 percent of mechanical engineers, 8 percent of university teachers, and 19 percent of doctors.

Protestants dominated the local government and the Royal Ulster Constabulary (RUC)—the police. Northern Ireland received millions of pounds a year from the British government to invest in infrastructure, but a disproportionate amount of this money went to Protestant areas.

One group that did not accept Northern Ireland's status was the Irish Republican Army (IRA). Remnants of this organization had existed ever since the Civil War, even though the Free State had outlawed it. From 1956 to 1962, IRA terrorists in the Republic waged a guerrilla war across the border against Northern Ireland's police force and soldiers. The conflict claimed nineteen lives. In the end, however, the IRA ceased the effort after it acknowledged that it had no support from the people of either the Republic or Northern Ireland.

In the late 1960s, the Catholic minority of Northern Ireland was kept as an underclass by an entrenched system of discrimination in employment, housing, and education. Anger at the continuing inequality would spark a wave of civil rights protests. These protests set in motion the bloody conflict known as the Troubles.

For more than three decades, the Troubles have raged in Northern Ireland. By 1999, they had claimed the lives of 3,636 people and injured 36,000 more. Most of those people were civilians. The recent success of the peace process, however, suggests that Ireland may be ready to leave tragedy behind.

## 89 } Sunday, Bloody Sunday

In the late 1960s, a population of young, educated, and unemployed Catholics looked west and saw the success of the Civil Rights movement in the United States. They created the Northern Ireland Civil Rights Association (NICRA), intending to use peaceful protest to bring attention to discrimination in employment and housing.

One of NICRA's first efforts at peaceful protest was the Derry March of 1968, which many people consider the start of the Troubles. The protesters planned to march from Belfast to Derry, imitating Martin Luther King's 1966 march from Selma to Montgomery. The 600 marchers proceeded peacefully for four days, but when they reached Derry, a mob of Protestants attacked them with stones, nails, and crowbars. The RUC escort—which was composed primarily of Protestants—did little to protect them. Riots broke out in the Catholic Bogside neighborhood, which the RUC put down brutally.

The Derry March was an inauspicious beginning to the Unionist-Republican debate. It established an unfortunate precedent of mass violence between the sides, and it told the Catholic population that it could not trust the RUC to look after its safety. When Protestant paramilitary groups subsequently launched campaigns of arson and intimidation against them, the Catholics turned to a group that was more than willing to fight back—the IRA.

The IRA had kept calling for a united Ireland since the War of Independence, although its agitation hadn't been taken seriously for years. The outbreak of violence in Derry was exactly what its members had been looking for: an excuse to strike back at the Unionists and the police forces, which the IRA saw as the agents of British imperialism.

The IRA took on the role of police and defense force for Northern Ireland's Catholics. If someone sold drugs in a Catholic neighborhood, he could be maimed or even killed by the IRA. If Unionist paramilitaries burned down a Catholic house, the IRA would bomb a Protestant pub.

A stream of guns and bombs started flowing into the neighborhoods of Belfast and Derry.

The Unionist paramilitaries, meanwhile, were waging their own campaign of terror. Groups like the Ulster Defence Association (UDA) and the Red Hand Commandoes used the same tactics of murder and bombing. The UDA's attacks were generally meant to intimidate activist Catholics or to retaliate for IRA killings, which were usually in retaliation for UDA murders, which were generally retaliations for earlier IRA murders . . . and so on.

Of the paramilitary groups, the IRA always received the lion's share of news coverage. There were two reasons for this. First, Irish descendants in other countries have tended to sympathize with the IRA cause, even while condemning its methods. The news plays to them. Second, the IRA chose the United Kingdom as its enemy, whereas the UDA targeted neighborhoods and individuals. When the British government tried to control the Troubles, it moved against the group that had targeted it—the IRA. This led to increasing coverage of the IRA's role in the conflict, and it also led many Catholics to perceive that the British government was biased against their side. This perception of British bias grew much worse after one of the most notorious events of the Troubles—Bloody Sunday.

To control the increasing power of the IRA, the British government sent its army into Northern Ireland and began a policy of internment. This meant that police or soldiers could seize a suspected terrorist without formal charges and hold him or her indefinitely. By 1972, hundreds of Irish Catholics were being detained on these terms.

NICRA protested internment by holding a march through Derry's Bogside neighborhood on January 30, 1972. The local RUC chief recommended that the march be allowed to proceed as planned. An unnamed authority, however, decided instead to use the event to send in British paratroopers to arrest IRA members.

The march went on as planned and was relatively uneventful until around 4 P.M., when the soldiers arrived. They moved past the barricades and opened fire on the crowd. The march immediately dispersed in panic, and the troops followed to pursue the "arrest operation." The precise order of events that followed has been disputed for the last three decades, but the indisputable fact is that the soldiers shot thirteen civilians dead on the spot and injured another man who later died of his wounds.

After the troops had moved out, British authorities immediately issued statements that the men killed were IRA members who had fired on the soldiers. But in the days that followed, these claims were retracted. Subsequent investigations determined that none of the men killed were carrying weapons. Investigations also failed to establish that there was any concentrated IRA presence at the scene or that the soldiers had been fired on first. What is clear is that not a single soldier was injured during the operation.

Bloody Sunday was the first time in the Troubles that British soldiers had opened fire at unarmed civilians. People throughout Ireland were outraged by the atrocity; on February 2, a mob attacked and burned the British embassy in Dublin, and in Australia, dockers refused to unload British cargo ships. The British government appointed Lord Widgery, lord chief justice of England, to investigate. Widgery determined that none of the victims could be proved to have had weapons and that while some of the soldiers might have acted irresponsibly, they did not act illegally. In compiling this report, Widgery reviewed the reports of soldiers and RUC officers but ignored the statements collected from more than 500 civilians at the scene. No soldiers were punished. The Widgery report was met with outrage—some even refer to it as the "Widgery Whitewash."

Bloody Sunday ignited Catholic fears of government bias. The British government decided that the situation in Northern Ireland had gone beyond the local government's ability to control. It suspended the Northern Ireland Parliament in Stormont and imposed direct rule from London. The fifty-year experiment in home rule was over.

## 90 } The Peace Process

By 1972, Northern Ireland was in chaos: the body count from paramilitary violence was rising daily, British soldiers were patrolling the streets, and the entire state was divided along seemingly unbridgeable social lines. The British government, faced with governing this mess, began proceedings to restore Northern Ireland home rule on more stable grounds.

It was a gargantuan political puzzle. Negotiators had to bring together Catholic and Protestant politicians who were increasingly at each other's throats.

The negotiators ironed out an agreement in December 1973 in Sunningdale, England. The principal point was the restoration of Northern

Ireland home rule, with power shared between Catholics and Protestants. It called for the creation of a Council of Ireland to promote cooperation between Northern Ireland and the Republic. The English agreed to release political prisoners and reform the RUC, while the Irish agreed to suppress the IRA and to scale back their claims to Northern Ireland. People hoped that the compromise agreement would allow for lasting peace.

Sadly, it was not to be. Unionist groups felt that the arrangement ceded too much to Catholics. The Ulster Workers' Council, a working-class Loyalist group, called a general strike in Belfast that lasted for thirteen days. The strike—and the paramilitary violence that accompanied it— brought Northern Ireland to a standstill. The local government decided to withdraw from the Sunningdale Agreement. The United Kingdom concluded that if it couldn't reform Northern Ireland, it would try to contain it. For the next two decades, Britain treated the Troubles as primarily a security problem with the IRA.

In the following decades, the Troubles remained a source of pain and dismay for rational people throughout the world. The cycle of killing, retaliation, and counterkilling continued despite all attempts to stop it. Britain discovered that it could patrol the streets and throw thousands in jail, but as long as there was an angry young Catholic with a gun or a bomb, the violence would continue. The Catholic minority learned that they could talk to the politicians all they wanted, but as long as the Protestant working class wanted to maintain its position of superiority, the intimidation would continue. A shadow had fallen over Northern Ireland.

One of the more notorious episodes of the Troubles was the so-called Dirty Protest of IRA prisoners. The IRA prisoners wanted to be treated like prisoners of war, which would allow them to wear their own clothes, but the British insisted that they were common criminals. To protest, the prisoners refused to wear prison clothes or to clean their cells. For months, they huddled under blankets, wallowing in filth. International journalists called their conditions appalling, but British Prime Minister Margaret Thatcher replied that if they chose to live in squalor, that was their problem.

In 1981, after it became clear that the dirty tactics wouldn't work, the prisoners adopted a more extreme approach. Bobby Sands, a charismatic twenty-seven-year-old prisoner, announced that he would not eat until he received prisoner-of-war status. Every ten days, a fellow prisoner joined him on the hunger strike. The British thought he was bluffing; Prime Minister Thatcher refused to give in to the moral blackmail tactics. The IRA's Gerry Adams pleaded with Sands to call off the strike, as did the Catholic bishop of Derry. While Sands wasted away, he won an election for Parliament as a Sinn Féin candidate.

But he never took his seat in Westminster. After sixty-six days without food, Bobby Sands, MP (member of Parliament), died. Riots struck throughout Belfast, and 100,000 people attended his funeral procession.

In the following months, nine more hunger strikers died. Finally, the prisoners called off the strike—they had decided not to lose any more lives in a futile gesture. Three days later, Britain granted the IRA prisoners most of their demands.

# 91⟩ The Good Friday Agreement

There was a glimmer of hope in 1985, when the United Kingdom and the Republic of Ireland tried to break through the deadlock of violence by clearing up their own interests in Northern Ireland. Prime Minister Thatcher and Garrett Fitzgerald, the *taoiseach* (Irish prime minister) signed the Anglo-Irish Agreement, which stated that "any change in the status of Northern Ireland would only come about with the consent of a majority of the people in Northern Ireland." It was a historic statement, making clear that Ulster's fate would be determined by democratic processes within Ulster, and only by those processes. The agreement also established an intergovernmental conference that gave the Republic an official consultative role in the affairs of Northern Ireland.

While the Anglo-Irish Agreement laid the grounds for peace as far as England and the Republic were concerned, it was not well received in Northern Ireland. Unionist MPs resigned in protest, and Unionist workers called a province-wide strike. The IRA wasn't impressed either; later that year, it issued a threat of violence against all civilians, Catholic or Protestant, who worked with the RUC. The following year, a massive IRA bomb killed eleven people at a Remembrance Day ceremony in Enniskillen. Peace was not at hand.

For decades, it seemed that the best anyone could hope for was a contained level of violence. But a spark of hope appeared in the early 1990s when Gerry Adams, head of the IRA's political arm Sinn Féin, revealed that he'd been in peace talks with John Hume, head of the Social Democratic Labour Party (SDLP), the moderate Catholic party.

If the IRA was ready to talk, perhaps there was a chance for peace.

In January 1994, President Bill Clinton granted Gerry Adams a visa to visit the United States for the first time; previous administrations had always banned Adams because of his associations with terrorists. Adams's visit was historic for two reasons. First, it allowed him to gather the political support of Irish-Americans, which increased Sinn Féin's status in later negotiations. Second, it forced him to act as a politician, rather than as a spokesman for terrorists. He knew that if he wanted to keep the support of the United States, he needed to exchange the rifle for the negotiating table.

The IRA declared a unilateral cease-fire on August 31, 1994. In October the Unionist paramilitaries followed suit. In 1995, representatives of the United Kingdom and Ireland met to iron out a framework for a peace settlement. The document they came up with called for points similar to the Sunningdale Agreement:

- Northern Ireland remained part of the United Kingdom, but only so long as the majority still desired it.
- Northern Ireland would return to a form of independent government.
- The parties would create a "north-south" body that (hopefully) would lead to stronger ties between the Republic and Northern Ireland.

The framework was not an actual settlement, nor was it popular with either Republicans or Unionists. Efforts to turn the framework into an actual settlement were slow. British Prime Minister John Major insisted that the peace process could move forward only if the IRA agreed to decommission their arms. Gerry Adams refused; he viewed Major's position as a trick to break the IRA's power without granting any concessions.

On February 9, 1996, the IRA announced its dissatisfaction with the process by exploding an immense bomb at Canary Wharf in London. The resumption of violence was met with appalled condemnation on all sides. The British government attacked the IRA and scored a number of successes. It appeared that the nasty conflict of the 1980s and early 1990s was back again.

Fortunately, two political changes in 1997 got the peace process back on track. First, Sinn Féin won its largest percentage of the vote ever, which many interpreted as popular support for a resolution of the conflict through peaceful means. Second, Labour Prime Minister Tony Blair swept into power with a crushing victory over the Conservatives. Blair immediately put out feelers to Sinn Féin to get the peace process started again.

After a touch-and-go period, Prime Minister Blair brought all the major parties together in 1998. Extremists on both sides threatened to scuttle the talks, but last-minute heroics by Blair, U.S. Senator George Mitchell, and President Bill Clinton kept the negotiators at the table. The

Good Friday Agreement of April 10, 1998, laid the groundwork for what many hope will be a lasting peace.

The Good Friday Agreement adopted many of the provisions of previous peace attempts, such as the Sunningdale Agreement. One of the unfortunate ironies of the situation is that it took so long to reach essentially the same solution as was rejected in 1974. But maybe it took years of violence to make people accept the necessary compromises:

- Home rule returned to Northern Ireland, with a representative assembly sharing power between Catholics and Protestants.
- The RUC was reorganized and renamed the Police Service of Northern Ireland.
- The IRA and UDA agreed to maintain the cease-fire.
- Assuming the cease-fire held, the IRA and UDA agreed to a gradual process of decommissioning their weapons.
- Political prisoners were released.
- The Republic of Ireland amended its constitution to remove its territorial claim to Northern Ireland until the people of Northern Ireland agreed to rejoin.

To go into effect, the agreement required the approval of a majority of the people in Northern Ireland and the Republic. In a May 1998 referendum, it drew the support of 94.4 percent of voters in the Republic and 71.1 percent of people in Northern Ireland. While this result gave a great boost to the peace process, one element of the vote still gave people pause—while 96 percent of Catholic voters in Northern Ireland supported the Good Friday Agreement, only 52 percent of Protestants voted in favor.

Today, the peace process continues to move forward. Catholics and Protestants share power, the RUC has been reorganized and renamed the Police Service of Northern Ireland, and the paramilitary groups have demonstrated a commitment, however reluctant, to put their weapons away for good. But it's been a rocky path, and the road ahead does not look much smoother.

Thirteen weeks after the Good Friday Agreement was reached, disaster struck. A Republican splinter group calling itself the Real IRA detonated a massive bomb in the Northern Ireland town of Omagh. Its death toll of twenty-eight was the largest single loss of life in the entire conflict.

If the bomb had gone off five years earlier, it would most likely have launched a wave of attacks and counterattacks—this is almost certainly what the Real IRA intended. But this time, the UDA and the IRA both kept the cease-fire. Gerry Adams released a statement condemning the attack, saying that "violence must be a thing of the past." The peace had passed its first major test.

Sadly, it wasn't the last test. Although the leaders have decided to move forward, there is still a great deal of anger left in the people of Northern Ireland. Every summer the peace gets tested in the Marching Season, when the Orange Order and Apprentice Boy parades antagonize Catholic neighborhoods. These are Unionist groups that march through

Catholic neighborhoods on dates significant to their history, such as the Protestant victory in the Battle of the Boyne.

## 92 } Ireland's Celtic Tiger

Historically, Ireland has been poor. In the Middle Ages, visitors were often shocked at the almost Stone Age poverty of many Irish farmers. In Victorian times, English visitors were appalled to learn that conditions had not improved much since medieval days. Even in the 1950s, the per-capita income of rural Irish citizens was less than one-third of the average for Europe. To many observers, it seemed that poverty was Ireland's natural state.

If those observers could have jumped ahead to the year 2003, they would have been stunned by the transformation. From the 1960s to the 1980s, Ireland experienced a series of economic growth spurts, which kicked into high gear in the mid-1990s. After several consecutive years of leading Europe in economic growth, Ireland now has one of the better standards of living in the world. This extraordinary development has earned Ireland the name "Celtic Tiger."

As with all macroeconomic questions, the answer is multifaceted and ambiguous, but a few key factors stand out. The first is Irish participation in the European Economic Community (EEC) and its successor organization, the European Union (EU). Since Ireland joined the EEC in 1972, it has been the single largest net recipient of EEC and EU funds—over

£20 billion to date. The EU follows a policy of supporting less prosperous member nations to help them reach the economic levels of wealthier members. Ireland used this money to build roads, update utilities, build up a tourism infrastructure, and subsidize agriculture. Ireland is small and the money was generally well spent, so the investments have made a noticeable impact on many people's lives.

International business investment was the next major reason for Ireland's success. The Irish government has gone out of its way to lure American and European businesses with tax breaks and incentive packages. The Republic of Ireland (which excludes Northern Ireland) is now an extremely safe place with very little crime, essentially no chance of war, and a stable government. The Republic has few large businesses of its own, so it is unlikely to initiate costly tariffs to protect native industry. Finally, the Republic of Ireland is an excellent place to locate an operation that does business in both Europe and North America, both because of its physical location and because it has a large percentage of bilingual English speakers.

## 93 } Ireland and the European Union

Participation in the EU has had extraordinary consequences for the Republic of Ireland. It led to the economic boom that the Irish have enjoyed, but those economic changes haven't made everyone happy. EU membership opens up to Irish businesses the giant market of European consumers, but it also means that the Republic of Ireland's weaker industries are now exposed to international competition. Traditional dairy farms, for example, simply can't compete with industrialized factory farms. Europe and the Republic of Ireland have so far supported these farmers with subsidies, but there is substantial pressure for the Irish agricultural industry to modernize itself to compete on the free market.

Another major impact of Europe has been on social issues. Traditionally, the Republic of Ireland has been a very conservative country, with close ties to the Catholic Church. Prevailing attitudes on the Continent have taken a much more liberal direction on issues like women's rights, abortion, and divorce. Although the Irish government has dragged its heels, international pressure and the will of the Irish people have forced it to liberalize many laws.

One of the more controversial issues for the Republic of Ireland is how its traditional stance of neutrality figures into EU membership. While the EU is not primarily a military organization, it does require a form of military alliance from its members. Concerns over possible future military entanglements led a majority of Irish voters to reject the EU Nice Treaty in 2001 (the Treaty opens EU membership to ten Eastern European countries that are possibly less stable than the current Western European members). After the Republic of Ireland's politicians spent a year promoting the treaty and wrangled some legal concessions out of EU bureaucrats, voters passed the treaty in a second referendum in 2002.

# 94 } Modern Irish Politics

The last forty years have been a tumultuous time for Irish politics. A series of governments in the 1970s and 1980s fell because they couldn't end the violence in the North or fix the Republic of Ireland's persistent unemployment. In addition, thorny social problems and an abundance of scandals made a rocky path for Irish politicians. Fortunately, matters seem to have improved in the 1990s.

No political issue in Ireland has aroused as much emotion as the question of the North. The Fianna Fáil Party, Ireland's dominant political party throughout the century, was founded on the premise that Ireland should never have been divided. After the issue nearly tore the country apart in the 1920s, politicians placed it on the backburner as a continuing source of grievance. De Valera's constitution of 1937 even laid claim to the territory as part of the Republic. In the following three decades, however, most people accepted that the North belongs to the United Kingdom.

When the Troubles erupted in the North, many people in the Republic had deeply conflicting feelings. On the one hand, they wanted to side with their Catholic brethren in Ulster, but on the other, they didn't want to disrupt their own country or their peaceful relationship with the United Kingdom. A crisis broke out in 1971 when two Cabinet ministers, including the future taoiseach Charles Haughey, were implicated in a scheme to smuggle weapons to Northern Catholics. The ministers resigned, but the question remained of how far the Republic should involve itself in the crisis.

In the end, the Republic wound up siding with Britain—both nations agreed that they would rather see an end to the violence than press their respective territorial claims. In 1985, they signed the Anglo-Irish Agreement, a framework for a peace settlement. Unfortunately, combatants in the North refused to give up the fight.

Irish leaders continued to try to end the violence. In 1998 Bertie Ahern, the leader of Fianna Fáil and the Irish taoiseach, took part in the Good Friday Peace Talks that finally brought a lasting peace agreement. Ahern brought back a referendum for the Irish people to approve the agreement, specifically the Republic of Ireland's rejection of its historical claim to Northern Ireland. The referendum passed by a wide margin. The question of the North is by no means answered for good, but for the first time in many years people believe that it's moving in the right direction.

In recent decades, a series of political scandals has significantly reduced the faith of the Irish in their leaders. Many of these scandals took place during the administration of Charlie Haughey, son-in-law to the legendary Fianna Fáil leader Sean Lemass, who had dominated Irish politics in the 1950s. Haughey had already been implicated in a smuggling scandal in 1971, but he somehow managed to clear his name and rise up to lead Fianna Fáil from 1979 to 1992, serving as taoiseach for several of those years.

The voters liked Haughey, but a shadow of corruption always seemed to follow his administration. The police force had a series of scandals under the Haughey regime. Several government departments experienced financial scandals, which somehow never implicated Haughey himself. The worst crisis came when it was discovered that Haughey's supporters had been wire-tapping journalists hostile to his administration; it was an Irish form of Watergate. Somehow, Haughey's popularity with the Fianna Fáil faithful kept him in charge of the party until 1992, when a biting investigation into corruption in the beef industry finally did him in.

Shadows of corruption still haunt the Irish political system, but there have been relatively few major crises in the last decade. It seems that current politicians are either more honest or more discreet.

The Irish political structure continues to be something of an anomaly, since the two dominant parties are divided less by ideology than by historical associations. Fianna Fáil, the party founded by Éamon de Valera and the forces who opposed the Anglo-Irish Treaty, has been the dominant party throughout the century. Fine Gael, the organization that emerged from the Free State politicians who supported the treaty, has managed to take control of the government on a number of occasions with the help of third parties. The major political parties in Ireland today are:

- Fianna Fáil—the original anti-treaty party
- Fine Gael—the original pro-treaty party

- ☘ **Labour**—a liberal workers' party
- ☘ **Progressive Democrats**—an offshoot of Fianna Fáil that is economically conservative and socially liberal; it has allied with Fine Gael at times
- ☘ **Democratic Left**—the modern incarnation of the original Sinn Féin; leftist but no longer socialist
- ☘ **Greens**—an environmental party

# 95 } The Liberalization of Ireland

Throughout the twentieth century, Ireland was known for its conservative social policies. When the rest of Europe was adopting liberal measures, Ireland held a firm stance against contraception, abortion, and divorce. These stances were inextricably linked to the close connection between the Roman Catholic Church and the Irish government. The early leaders of the Irish Free State wanted it that way; they consciously sought connections with the Catholic hierarchy in order to help establish the legitimacy of their government with the Irish people.

Ireland held firm to its traditional values for most of the century, but the winds of change blew in with the 1960s. When Ireland began to establish closer ties with the EEC and EU, many Irish people began to think their laws should be more in line with the general trends of European progressive values. The rise of feminist thought provided counterpoints to many of the patriarchal values of the Irish government.

Catholics are taught that sexual intercourse should take place only for the purpose of procreation; the use of contraceptives to prevent conception is an immoral act. For decades, the government of Ireland made it illegal to import or sell contraceptives. In 1966, however, the United Nations declared it a basic human right for an individual to control his or her own fertility. Although the government resisted this idea, many Irish people—particularly women—agreed.

There were numerous cases of Irish families who had been reduced to poverty by having more children than they could support, or of women whose health was wrecked by having ten or even twenty children. Public opinion decided that if family planning could improve people's lives, then it wasn't immoral. In the late 1960s doctors began prescribing birth control pills to married women, ostensibly for health reasons. In the early 1970s it became legal for married couples to buy condoms, provided they had a prescription. Over the next two decades the laws were relaxed to the point where people can now purchase condoms in vending machines.

The struggle over abortion has been one of the most acrimonious issues in contemporary Irish politics. Abortion has never been legal in Ireland (except in cases where the mother's life is at risk), and that does not appear likely to change in the near future. The controversy has been over whether women should be allowed to travel abroad for abortions, and whether they should be able receive information about it from medical professionals. Although it is difficult to get exact statistics, it is thought that a few thousand women every year travel to England to get abortions.

For the most part, the Irish government has been willing to ignore this practice.

In 1992, however, a case exploded that could not be ignored. A fourteen-year-old girl referred to as "X" by the media was raped by a family acquaintance and became pregnant. Her parents planned to take her to England for an abortion, but they wanted to bring back fetal tissue to use in the prosecution of their daughter's assailant. When they asked the police about this, the police turned the issue over to the district attorney's office, which declared that the girl could not leave the country specifically to receive an abortion. The parents sued for the right to take her abroad.

The conflict created a national scandal. Although most Irish people opposed abortion in most situations, they generally supported the girl's right to end a pregnancy that seemed so wrong. European Union officials complained that a free government did not have the right to inhibit its citizens' travel in that way. Eventually, government officials allowed her to leave under the pretext that the girl was suicidal, thereby allowing the traditional exception concerning the life of the mother.

The issue wasn't over. In 1993, conservative leaders proposed a constitutional change that would have made it illegal for women to travel abroad for abortions. The referendum failed, but it's interesting to note that 40 percent of voters supported the amendment. For the time being, the situation is much like it was before Case X, with thousands of women traveling to England for secret abortions.

Divorce has been another political hotspot in recent years. The Catholic Church opposes divorce on the grounds that marriage is a lifelong sacrament. While the Church does allow annulments—an official declaration that the marriage never took place—the policy has been unwieldy in practice and does not resolve the tricky legal disputes that divorces create. The legal complications have been one of the main reasons why Ireland has opposed divorce; in a country where the family farm is paramount and the husband owns all property by default, the government has been reluctant to tackle the issue of community property.

Over the last few decades, however, it became clear that Ireland had thousands of broken marriages, just like every other country in Europe.

It seemed to many people that Ireland was dodging the problem by declaring that it didn't exist. In 1986 the country held a referendum to make divorce legal, but it failed by a fairly substantial vote. In 1996, pressured by EU policies on divorce and property rights, Ireland held a second referendum, which passed by a tiny margin. Divorce is now legal, but there are still many people who view it as the wrong decision.

# 96} Women's Rights

One remarkable feature of modern Irish politics has been the advance of women to high offices. The seventh and eighth presidents of Ireland have been women. While this role has primarily been a figurehead office for most of its existence, Mary Robinson and Mary McAleese have redefined the position into a platform of international significance.

## MARY ROBINSON

Mary Robinson was born in Ballina, County Mayo, in 1944. She earned law degrees from Trinity College and Harvard University, and in 1969 she became Trinity College's youngest law professor ever. She became involved in Irish politics early, representing the Labour Party in the Irish Upper House of Parliament from 1969 to 1989. In 1988 she and her husband, Nicholas, founded the Irish Centre for European Law.

Robinson served as president of Ireland from 1990 to 1997. She pursued economic, political, and cultural ties with other nations, continuing Ireland's tradition of active involvement in the European Union. But Robinson didn't only seek to advance Ireland's ties to its wealthy neighbors; she also used the post to advocate the rights of poor countries throughout the world. Citing Ireland's experiences in the Great Famine, she argued for the responsibilities of industrialized nations to help developing nations.

Robinson brought this sense of international responsibility to the United Nations, where she served as high commissioner for human rights from June 1997 to September 2002. Robinson used the relatively obscure position to take strong stances on human rights issues around the world. She traveled to dozens of nations during her term. Her condemnation of human rights abuses in China and Chechnya aroused defensive reactions from the Chinese and Russian leaders. She created more surprise by criticizing NATO bombing in Serbia and U.S. bombing campaigns in Afghanistan.

Robinson has won the Fulbright Prize for International Understanding and the Indira Gandhi Peace Prize.

### MARY MCALEESE

Mary McAleese was born in 1951 to a Catholic family in Belfast. She became aware of Northern Ireland's problems at an early age, when her father's shop was fired on in sectarian violence. Her early career was similar in some ways to Mary Robinson's; she earned a law degree at Queens University and became a law professor at Trinity College. McAleese has served on several legal committees in Ireland, and in 1987 she became pro-vice chancellor of Queens University, the first woman to hold that role. She has also been an active broadcaster with Radio Telefís Éireann.

McAleese took office as the eighth president of Ireland in November 1997, the first person from Northern Ireland to serve in this role. "Building Bridges" has been the theme of her presidency—she has sought to promote social inclusion, equality, and reconciliation throughout Ireland. Many people hope that her inclusive philosophy will help build a stronger relationship between the North and the South.

The face of Ireland is changing. The charming but patronizing images of the past—the simple farmer, the friendly drunk—have given way to the real faces of Seamus Heaney, U2's Bono, and Mary Robinson. Europe's perennially poor cousin has become the Celtic Tiger.

## 97 } Family Life

The Irish have used the strengths of their island—the fresh food and water, the tranquility, and the strong family connections—to create one of the most enjoyable lifestyles in the world.

It's difficult to make general statements about the family life of any country. People's lives can be very different, depending on where they live or how much money they have. Even people living next door to each other can lead very different lives. That being said, there are a few traits that people have accepted as describing the traditional Irish family.

The stereotypical Irish family is Roman Catholic. Catholic roots go very deep in Ireland—so deep that they were able to withstand hundreds of years of English opposition. Irish households have traditionally been full of Catholic art and objects, and most Irish children have been educated at Catholic schools. The influence of the Church has tended to make Ireland a conservative country; the government has generally sided with Church positions on issues like abortion, divorce, and contraception.

The stereotypical Irish Catholic family is large, with many children close in age. Late marriage and abstinence have decreased family size in the 150 years since the Great Famine, but the twentieth century saw enough large Irish Catholic families to keep the image alive. Partially responsible for this phenomenon is the Catholic prohibition of contraception.

The Irish have long been seen as a pastoral people with strong connections to their families and community. When most people worked in agriculture, their lives were very much tied to the land. They worked long hours, lived in the same houses that their parents had lived in, and rarely traveled more than 10 miles from home. This lifestyle offered few luxuries, but it fostered strong family and community networks.

Economic modernization has caused many Irish people to move from the country to pursue jobs in the cities. This has resulted in a quantitative increase in the quality of life for most people, but also a disruption in the traditional community networks. Many young people relish the chance to escape from the farm or small town and earn money in the city, and they willingly cast off what they see as the shackles of religion.

## 98 } Irish Food: Potatoes, Beef, and More Potatoes—and a Cuppa!

The Irish family has traditionally gathered around the table, sharing the food it had in rich times and in poor. For the most part, it has been pretty decent fare. Ireland's thriving agricultural industry provides high-quality meat, dairy products, and vegetables that go directly to local markets. The fresh and nutritious ingredients have allowed the Irish population to stay remarkably healthy, even in times of relative poverty.

Irish food has never been known for its diversity. The traditional diet, consisting of meat, vegetables, and lots and lots of potatoes, has long been considered one of the blandest in Europe. What it lacks in flair, though, it makes up in heartiness. Some of Ireland's substantial national and regional dishes include the following:

- **Blaa** ("blah")—sausage rolls, from Waterford
- **Coddle**—boiled sausages and bacon with potatoes, from Dublin
- **Colcannon**—a casserole of potatoes, onions, and cabbage
- **Crubeen**—pig's feet, from Cork
- **Guinness stew**—a stew made with mutton, potatoes, carrots, and Guinness beer
- **Soda bread**—a thick brown bread, tasty when fried

The Irish tend to eat light lunches, so they take breakfast seriously. Visitors to Ireland are frequently amazed by the robust Irish breakfast. This is no dainty continental breakfast of a croissant and jam, but an extravaganza of meat and eggs that will keep you full all day. There is variation from place to place, but the Irish breakfast generally includes the following:

- Eggs (usually fried)
- White pudding (a lighter sausage)
- Sausages
- Fried tomatoes
- Bacon (sliced thick)
- Toast and jam

- ♣ Ham
- ♣ Tea
- ♣ Black pudding (a blood sausage)

This combination is served in pubs and bed-and-breakfasts across the country. A similar variant, called an "Ulster Fry," is served in the North. Observant visitors will notice that the Irish don't actually eat like this every day; a bowl of cereal or some toast and tea are more common ways to start the day.

It's hard to overestimate the importance of tea in Irish culture. Tea is simultaneously a beverage, a medicine, and a social ritual. The Irish drink on average four cups of tea a day, amounting to 7 pounds of dried tea leaves over the course of a year—easily the highest rate of per-capita tea consumption in the world. No respectable household would be found without tea, and pubs are legally required to provide it. At breakfast, lunch, and teatime (approximately 4 P.M.), tea is the beverage of choice.

The Anglo-Irish aristocracy introduced tea to Ireland in the nineteenth century. As an import from India, it was too expensive for most Irish people at first, but lower prices and generally improving economic conditions allowed more and more people to try this new taste sensation. Soon the whole nation was hooked. (They pronounced the name of their new drink "tay," from the French pronunciation.)

A cup of tea is often referred to as a "cuppa"—everyone knows what kind of cup you're talking about. People throughout the country take a break in the mid-afternoon to enjoy a cup of tea and some light snacks such as cookies or finger sandwiches. The Irish drink tea with sugar and generous amounts of milk. Tea devotees extol the drink's powers to aid digestion, cure headaches, and provide a gentle pick-me-up.

The Irish tend to prefer stronger tea than the English—they have a saying that a good cup of tea should be "strong enough for a mouse to trot on." They've gravitated toward East African suppliers, who provide more aromatic leaves. Irish tea was traditionally made using free leaves, but in recent decades consumers have grown more accepting of tea bags. The Irish maintain very high standards for their tea; consequently, the quality of tea in Ireland is generally much higher than in the United States.

The Irish initially relied entirely on U.K. importers for their tea supply, which became a problem during World War II, when Ireland chose not to ally itself with the United Kingdom. Consequently, the government of Ireland set up Tea Importers (Éire), Ltd., a conglomeration of companies that imported tea directly from the producing countries.

Irish tea consumption continued to increase in the postwar years. In 1973 Ireland had to disband Tea Importers because it violated antimonopoly statutes of the EU, so the business was taken up by the subsidiary companies that had made up the organization.

# 99 } For the Love of Irish Beer and Whiskey

Pubs play a very important role in Irish life. American visitors tend to assume that pubs are the same thing as bars, but this isn't exactly true. Pubs do sell alcohol, but they also serve as restaurants, music stages, meeting places, and even as local cultural museums. Most pubs aren't all these things simultaneously, but instead specialize in one area.

One thing that often surprises visitors is the presence of children and families in Irish pubs. The drinking age in Ireland is eighteen, but it's legal for children under that age to enter with their families. The families are there for the music or the food. Irish pub food—called "pub grub"—is generally inexpensive and hearty. While almost any pub can be expected to provide sandwiches or maybe a baked potato, some pubs have become famous for their food; The Reginald in Waterford, The Stag's Head in Dublin, and Langton's in Kilkenny are good places to visit for Irish culinary delights.

Pubs are the places to go for traditional music, or "trad," as the locals call it. Larger places might bring in professional bands, but the most common format is the session, in which local musicians come with what instruments they have and just get down to business. The musicians in a session are usually playing for beer only, so there generally isn't a cover charge. The pubs in Doolin are famous for their trad.

Ireland has one of the highest beer consumption rates in the world. The unique thing about Irish beer habits is that the most popular type of beer is stout, whereas all other European markets prefer lagers or ales. The most famous stout, of course, is Guinness.

If you stop at a pub in Ireland and ask for a pint, the bartender will invariably bring you a Guinness. This unspoken understanding demonstrates the centrality of Guinness in Irish pub culture. Guinness stout is not only the national drink, it is also one of Ireland's leading exports; in recent years Guinness has sold close to 2 billion pints of stout per year in more than 150 different countries.

Arthur Guinness started the first Guinness brewery in 1759 with the help of a £100 inheritance from his godfather, the archbishop of Cashel. A man with vision, Guinness took out a 9,000-year lease on a run-down brewery on St. James Street in Dublin, right next to the Liffey River. This location was crucial, because it ensured a ready supply of pure Irish spring water. Guinness was a big fan of porter, as stout was called then, and he dedicated his new brewery to producing it. After some experimentation he found a taste that people loved, and the business has been growing ever since.

Like all beers, Guinness is made from barley, hops, yeast, and water (originally from the St. James wells in County Kildare). Guinness's distinctive flavor and dark color come from the practice of roasting the hops before brewing them. The beer isn't black, as many people think, but actually a deep ruby color—you can see the true color by holding your pint up to the light.

A proper pint of Guinness should have a thick head of foam on top. To get this right, the bartender pours the draft into the pint, lets it sit for three or four minutes, then tops it off for serving. Traditionally, Guinness stout was served at room temperature. (Irish room temperature can be pretty cool, so that doesn't mean the beer was warm.) Some pubs in Ireland continue that practice. There used to be a big difference between the flavors of draft Guinness and bottled Guinness, but recent advances in packaging technology have produced cans that can pour a pint almost as good as you'd find in a pub in County Meath.

With Guinness stout's strong flavor and popularity, it was inevitable that people would think of innovative ways to serve it. There are now many mixed drinks involving Guinness. Here are some of the more popular variants:

- **Black and Tan**—Guinness and a lager or pale ale (traditionally Bass Ale)
- **Black Velvet**—Guinness and champagne
- **Snakebite**—Guinness and cider
- **Purple Meany**—Guinness and a bitter
- **Drop of Diesel**—a shot of Guinness in a pint of Smithwicks ale

The most popular pint, of course, is pure draught Guinness. There is considerable dispute in Ireland about where you can find the best pint. In Dublin, the two leading contenders are the St. James Gate Brewery and Mulligan's, a nearby pub that, according to folklore, has a pipe connecting its basement to the brewery. Other Irish people claim that you'll find the best pint in little pubs out in the country that serve their beer at room temperature and never clean the tap.

Guinness gets the lion's share of attention, but there are a number of other excellent Irish beers. Brewers in Cork make Murphy's and Beamish, stouts that appear similar to Guinness but have distinctly different flavors. In Cork and the rest of Munster, these local brews are often more popular than Guinness stout. You can occasionally find Murphy's in bars outside of Ireland.

Smithwicks ("Smiddicks") is the local brew in Kilkenny. Smithwicks is an amber ale with a slightly hoppy flavor. It's served throughout Ireland. In continental Europe, you might find it under the name "Kilkenny."

There are a number of other beers that have recently come on the market to take advantage of the international enthusiasm for Irish beer. Harp is a lager brewed by Guinness. Murphy's has started brewing an ale called Murphy's Irish Red. With the proliferation of Irish pubs around the world, expect more Irish beers to appear in the near future.

Queen Elizabeth I of England once remarked that her only true Irish friend was whiskey. The word "whiskey" comes from the Gaelic words *uisce beatha*, which mean "water of life." The origins of whiskey are lost in the mists of time; some historians think the distilling technology was developed in the Far East and brought to Scotland and Ireland by traveling Celts. By 1000 C.E. people in both Scotland and Ireland were fermenting grains, distilling the brew, and aging the final product in wooden barrels.

Modern Irish whiskey is similar to Scotch whisky, but it's distilled three times instead of two, it's slightly sweeter, has less peat flavor, and it's spelled with an "e"—Scotch is spelled "whisky." Although Scotch whisky enjoys a far larger market today, in the nineteenth century Irish whiskey was the more popular drink. It was the liquor of choice in Victorian England, but in the period from 1910 to 1945 the Irish whiskey industry hit on hard times when the combination of Irish independence, American Prohibition, trade disputes with England, and World War II effectively ruined the export market.

Nevertheless, the domestic Irish market managed to keep a few distillers alive. The Bushmill's distillery in the North continued to produce Bushmill's malt whiskey, and the Midleton distillery near Cork produced the Jameson, Powers, and Midleton whiskies.

In recent years, Ireland's tourist boom has encouraged entrepreneurs to revive old Irish brands and distilleries. Today, there are dozens of Irish whiskey brands on the market, like Paddy, Kilbeggan, Locke's, Tullamore Dew, Redbreast, and Greenore.

A discussion of Irish distilled beverages would not be complete without a mention of poteen, *poitín* (po-CHEEN) in Irish Gaelic, an extremely strong grain alcohol made in unlicensed stills in the country—like moonshine. It's said that farmers used to give *poitín* to cows in labor. Supposedly, you can still find it in remote rural areas, but we don't recommend that you drink it; the ethyl alcohol in bad batches can be poisonous.

For better or worse, alcohol is an important part of Irish life. Irish beer and whiskey provide jobs for thousands of people, they pump export money into the economy, and they help create the boisterous pub atmosphere that is such a big part of Irish life. The unfortunate side effect of this success is the high rate of alcoholism in the Irish population. Ireland has consistently had one of the highest alcohol consumption rates in Europe; in 2000, the average Irish person consumed 12.3 liters of pure alcohol. This tradition of excess has taken its toll in lost productivity, lives cut short, and a reputation for drunkenness that has been hard to shake.

The stereotype of the drunken Irishman has a complicated history. Some aspects of Irish culture have tended to promote alcohol consumption: the long-standing heritage in producing beer and whiskey, the desire to escape from continuing poverty and oppression, and the relatively benign view that the Catholic Church has tended to take on alcohol. But while the stereotype has probably been backed up by elements of truth, it is also true that it was often perpetuated by politicians who wanted to suppress Irish political power. Anti-Irish and anti-Catholic politicians in England and the United States frequently evoked the image of the drunken Irishman to stir up animosity against the Irish.

The Republic of Ireland has fought to bring down alcoholism and the stereotype that goes with it. Government actions have increased the penalties for drunk driving, limited the hours that pubs can be open, and mandated that pubs must serve nonalcoholic beverages. Public education campaigns have helped reduce some of the worst consequences of drinking, but the overall rate of consumption is still high. How Ireland will deal with this issue in the future remains to be seen.

# 100 } Irish Contributions to Literature and Art

Irish writers have made extraordinary contributions to English literature, and include four Nobel Prize winners. Although many of Ireland's greatest writers left their island to work in other countries, their work demonstrates the love of wit and poetry that has characterized the Irish people for centuries.

The full story of Irish literature begins long before the English ever arrived in Ireland. The Celtic epics described earlier, such as the *Táin Bó Cuailnge*, represent one of the great oral literary traditions in world history. In the Middle Ages, Irish bards were famous for the originality of their poetry. It is very unfortunate that relatively little of that poetry survives today.

Few Irish writers stood out during the years of English domination. After all, most of the Irish were uneducated farmers who had little opportunity to express themselves in writing. Moreover, the most talented writers went to England to pursue the greater opportunities there. This trend of writers leaving the country has continued into the modern day, but within the last 150 years the growth of Irish consciousness has created a greater distinction between the cultures of Ireland and England, in the minds of both the Irish and the rest of the world. This distinction has allowed people to talk about a body of Irish literature that can stand shoulder-to-shoulder with the literature of England or the United States.

Irish writers often receive literary awards for which they compete with writers from all over the world. In the last century, four Irish writers won the Nobel Prize in literature:

- ☘ William Butler Yeats, 1923
- ☘ George Bernard Shaw, 1925
- ☘ Samuel Beckett, 1969
- ☘ Seamus Heaney, 1995

## Jonathan Swift (1667–1745)

Ireland's first great contributor to English literature was Jonathan Swift. Born in Dublin to Protestant English parents, Swift faced financial challenges after his father's early death. After an education at Trinity College, he moved to London to serve as secretary to Sir William Temple. With Temple's help, Swift obtained appointments with the Church of England in both England and Ireland. In 1713 he became the dean of Saint Patrick's Cathedral in Dublin, where he remained for the rest of his life; when historians of the Protestant Ascendancy refer to "the dean," they are talking about Swift.

## OSCAR WILDE (1854–1900)

Oscar Wilde was born into a house where his creativity could reign free: his father was a famously eccentric surgeon, while his mother, "Speranza" Wilde, was a well-known socialite and writer of nationalist poetry. With his privileged background, Wilde was able to study at Oxford, where he became a disciple of Walter Pater and led the aesthetic movement, in which he advocated the idea of "art for art's sake."

Unfortunately, tragedy brought him down. Wilde was a homosexual, and he had carried on an affair with Lord Alfred Douglas for some time. Douglas's father, the marquis of Queensberry, accused Wilde of committing sodomy, a crime in Victorian England. Wilde sued the marquis for libel, but after a sensational trial Wilde was convicted and sentenced to two years of hard labor. His incarceration left him physically, financially, and spiritually ruined. He fled to Paris, where he died, broken and penniless, in 1900.

## WILLIAM BUTLER YEATS (1865–1939)

W. B. Yeats is widely considered to be one of the greatest poets of the twentieth century. He was born in Dublin in 1865 to an Anglo-Irish landowning family. His father, John Butler Yeats, was a well-known painter. Yeats spent much of his childhood in County Sligo, in West Ireland. He pursued painting as a young man, but he soon decided that his true passion was poetry.

The first inspirations for Yeats's poetry were the landscape, language, and mythology of Sligo. The folktales he heard from the local people led him to develop a fascination with Celtic stories and mysticism that influenced his work throughout his life. In the 1880s he became one of the leading voices promoting the study of Irish language and folklore. His poems, such as "The Wanderings of Oisin" (1889) and "The Lake Isle of Innisfree" (1893), communicated his love of Celtic myth to a wider audience. Yeats was a prolific and versatile writer throughout his career. His work in drama, folklore, and essays would each independently have made him a luminary of Irish literature. His true genius, however, came out in his poetry. In 1923, the year the Irish Free State was declared, Yeats won the Nobel Prize in literature "for his always inspired poetry, which in a highly artistic form gives expression to the spirit of a whole nation."

## JAMES JOYCE (1882–1941)

Joyce revolutionized the novel, the short story, and modern literature as we know it. He was born in Dublin, the first of ten children in a Catholic family. His father was a civil servant whose poor financial judgment left the family impoverished for much of Joyce's youth. Joyce attended Dublin's fine Jesuit schools, which gave him a firm grounding in theology and classical languages—subjects that repeatedly appeared in his later work. The story of his early life and his intellectual rebellion against Catholicism and Irish Nationalism are told in the largely autobiographical novel *A Portrait of the Artist as a Young Man* (1916), originally published in 1904 as *Stephen Hero*.

Joyce spent seven years working on *Ulysses* (1922); once he finished writing it, he almost couldn't find anyone to publish it. Once it was published, Ireland and the United States immediately banned it as obscene, and most people who located copies found the writing nearly incomprehensible. Despite these obstacles, *Ulysses* has come to be generally recognized as the most influential English novel of the twentieth century.

### SAMUEL BECKETT (1906–1989)

Beckett was born in Dublin to a middle-class Protestant family. After an education at Trinity College, he moved to Paris, where he befriended James Joyce and became involved in the Parisian literary scene. Beckett experimented with various styles during this period, producing poems, novels, and short stories that were popular in French critical circles. During World War II, Beckett stayed in France and was active in the Resistance.

In the postwar years, Beckett began to find true success by evolving his own style and writing primarily in French (he usually translated the English versions himself). He wrote a critically acclaimed trilogy of novels: *Molloy, Malone Dies*, and *The Unnameable*. His greatest successes were his plays, particularly *Waiting for Godot* and *Endgame*. In 1969 Beckett received the Nobel Prize in literature "for his writing, which—in new forms for the novel and drama—in the destitution of modern man acquires its elevation" (in other words, for inventing absurdist drama). He produced a number of plays in the 1970s and 1980s, which were widely read but less original than his earlier works. He died in Paris in 1989.

### SEAMUS HEANEY: POET OF THE TROUBLES (1939– )

The American poet Robert Lowell said that Seamus Heaney is the greatest Irish poet since Yeats: Oddly, he was born in the year of Yeats's death. Heaney was the oldest of nine children in a Catholic farming family in County Derry, Northern Ireland. At St. Columb's College in Derry and Queens University in Belfast, Heaney received a grounding in Latin, Irish, and Anglo-Saxon that has enriched the language of his poetry. The themes of his poems arose from the tensions of the land in which he lived: Ulster's industrial present versus its rural past; English roots versus Gaelic; and the rising conflict between Northern Ireland's Catholics and Protestants.

Heaney has produced a number of vibrant poetry collections: *Death of a Naturalist* (1966), *North* (1975), *Station Island* (1984), and *Seeing Things* (1991). In addition, he has written plays, essays, and a bestselling translation of the Anglo-Saxon epic *Beowulf* (1999). Heaney received the 1995 Nobel Prize in literature "for works of lyrical beauty and ethical depth, which exalt everyday miracles and the living past."

# 101} TRACING YOUR ROOTS

The world is full of descendants of Irish emigrants. In the United States alone, some 42 million people are descended from Irish Catholic or Protestant immigrants. Most of these descendants know little more about their Irish roots than the names of their family and the county they came from. But more and more people are taking an interest in learning about Irish heritage, tracing their family histories, and even reaffirming ties to relatives back in the old country.

There are a number of family names that are widely known to be Irish. Some of them are very old indeed, dating back to the Celtic peoples who controlled the island many centuries ago. Other names were added later, as waves of invaders gradually merged with the Irish population. Thus, Irish surnames include Old Gaelic (O'Brien, O'Neill), Norman (FitzGerald, Butler), Scots (Hamilton), as well as a plethora of English names (White, Williamson).

About 10 percent of Irish surnames come from the Anglo-Normans of the twelfth and thirteenth centuries—the French, English, Welsh, and Flemish. A large proportion of surnames in the North come from Scotland, due to the Ulster Plantation in the 1600s. Furthermore, the English government Anglicized many old Irish surnames.

The prefix "O" means "descended from." Thus, someone named O'Grady is descended from an ancestor named Grady. Names beginning with this prefix are a dead giveaway that someone is of Irish descent. Sometimes the "O" gets dropped; if you want to look up a surname, check listings both with and without it—for example, when looking up the name O'Reilly, also check for "Reilly."

O'Brien is an illustrious name; this name supposedly comes in a direct line from Brian Boru, the great king of the eleventh century. Not all O'Briens are descendants of Brian Boru; some versions of the name are a corruption of O'Byrne or derive from the Norman surname Bryan. Many O'Briens come from County Clare or the town of Killaloe, where Brian Boru had a palace.

The name O'Connor also has a long history; it's a very old Gaelic surname. The O'Connors descended from King Conchobar of Connacht, who died in the tenth century. Roderick O'Connor was the last high king of Ireland. O'Connors became lords of Counties Mayo and Clare.

The O'Connors from County Offaly trace their descent to a king of Ireland from the second century C.E.; they fought hard against English rule in the 1500s and as a result were more or less destroyed as a wealthy dynasty, although the name did survive. O'Connors were a dominant family in County Sligo from the fourteenth to the seventeenth centuries, but lost all of their possessions after Cromwell.

The O'Donnells were prominent in County Donegal in the fourteenth century. One of their members, Red Hugh O'Donnell, was famous for his bravery fighting the English under Queen Elizabeth I. After Cromwell, the O'Donnells spread through Counties Mayo and Leitrim, and there are still many of them there, as well as in west Donegal. Many O'Donnells emigrated to the United States and Australia.

The O'Malleys were a famous seafaring family who controlled most of the west coast of Ireland from their base at Clew Bay in County Mayo. The name is still common in County Mayo. It was sometimes Anglicized to Melia.

O'Neill is one of the most common surnames in Ireland; it's among the ten most common names in Counties Antrim, Derry, and Tyrone. The O'Neills are descended from medieval kings of Ulster, who ruled the northern province for four centuries before being put down by the English. They controlled a number of other clans, but had the hardest time keeping their own rival factions of O'Neills living harmoniously. Hugh O'Neill was their last chief; in 1603, the English general Mountjoy destroyed the O'Neills coronation chair at Tullaghoge. Many O'Neills fled to Europe, especially Spain, where they flourished as statesmen and soldiers.

O'Reilly is another very common name, especially in the north; it's the most common name in Counties Cavan and Longford. In Irish it means "descendant of Raghallach" (one of the kings of Connacht). The O'Reillys were a warlike group known for their skill with cavalry. They were also successful medieval traders and produced a number of archbishops and bishops. They traced their descent to the fourth-century king Uí Briúin Breifne. They lost most of their property under Cromwell.

The name O'Rourke comes from "O'Ruairc," which means "descendant of Ruarc"; Ruarc comes from the Norse word *hrothekr*, or "famous king," a tenth-century king of Breifne. Variants on the name include O'Rorke, Rourke, Roark, and Rooke. The O'Rourkes also trace their ancestry to Brian, the fourth-century king of Connacht. The O'Rourkes fought the O'Connors for control of Connacht until the twelfth century, when the O'Connors won. They also fought with the O'Reillys. Their stronghold was in County Leitrim. Many O'Rourkes went to Europe after Cromwell confiscated their property, where they thrived in church and state; many of their descendants became important people in Poland and Russia.

Sullivan, or O'Sullivan, is another extremely common Irish surname. The name comes from the Gaelic Ó Suileabháin, which might mean "black-eyed," "hawk-eyed," or "one-eyed"—no one knows for sure. It is the most common surname in Munster, especially concentrated in Counties Cork and Kerry. The O'Sullivans were one of the most powerful families of the Eóghanacht in Munster. Most Irish Sullivans today have returned to the older form of O'Sullivan.

Many people are deeply curious about their family backgrounds. They want to know who their ancestors were, whether they did anything famous or infamous, and whether they were noble or peasant. Researching genealogy has long been a popular pastime. It's easier than ever to find ancestors now that the Internet and e-mail have made it possible to find documents or contact relatives with a click of a button.

Irish heritage can be a wonderful thing. Descendants of Irish emigrants can assure themselves that their ancestors came from a beautiful land with a vibrant culture and strong people. If your ancestors left their homeland under dire circumstances, you can assure yourself that they were tough enough to survive and carry on their names.

# Appendix A

# A Primer of the Irish Language

## IRISH PRONUNCIATION

Irish has three main dialects, Connacht, Munster, and Ulster; each of these has its own pronunciation quirks. Schools teach a standardized form of Irish that combines features of these three dialects.

### Vowels

Irish marks long vowels with an accent; short vowels have no accent. Here are the main vowel sounds:

a as in "bat"  
í as in "fee"  
á as "aw"  
o as in "son"  
e as in "pet"  

ó as in "glow"  
é as in "grey"  
u as in "took"  
i as in "hit"  
ú as in "rule"  

### Consonants

Irish has many clusters of consonants that have their own idiosyncratic pronunciations:

- **bh** as "v"
- **bhf** as "w"
- **c** as "k"
- **ch** as a guttural sound, like the "ch" in "Loch Ness"
- **d** as "d" when followed by a broad vowel, and as "j" when followed by a slender vowel

- **dh** as "g" when followed by a broad vowel, as "y" when followed by a slender vowel
- **mh** as "w"
- **s** as "s" before a broad vowel, as "sh" before a slender vowel or at the end of the word
- **t** as "t" before a broad vowel, as "ch" before a slender vowel
- **th** as the "h" in "house"; at the end of a word, either silent or pronounced as the "t" in "hat"

## Basic Words and Phrases

Here are a few common greetings and pleasantries:

**Please:** Le do thoil (le do hall)

**Thank you:** Go raibh maith agat (go rev mut agut)

**You're welcome:** Tá fáilte romhat (taw foil-cha row-ath) or just fáilte

**Hello** (to one person): Dia duit (dee-a gwit)

**Hello** (to several people): Dia daoibh (dee-a gweev)

**Hello** (in response to greeting): Dia's Muire duit (dee-as mwir-a gwit)

**Goodbye** (to a person leaving): Slán leat (slawn lath)

**Goodbye** (to a person staying behind): Slán agat (slawn agut)

**Goodnight:** Oíche mhaith (ee-ha ho)

**Cheers** (literally "health"): Sláinte (slan-chuh)

## Appendix B

# Irish Proverbs and Blessings

### IRISH PROVERBS

An Irishman is never drunk as long as he can hold on to one blade of grass and not fall off the face of the Earth.

A boy's best friend is his mother and there's no spancel stronger than her apron string. (A spancel is a rope used to tie up a sheep or other animal.)

A trout in the pot is better than a salmon in the sea.

If the knitter is weary the baby will have no new bonnet.

It's no use carrying an umbrella if your shoes are leaking.

If you lie down with dogs you'll rise with fleas.

Drink is the curse of the land.
It makes you fight with your neighbor.
It makes you shoot at your landlord—
and it makes you miss him!

## IRISH BLESSINGS

May the road rise to meet you.
May the wind be always at your back.
May the sun shine warm upon your face.
And rains fall soft upon your fields.
And until we meet again,
May God hold you in the hollow of His hand.

Leave the table hungry.
Leave the bed sleepy.
Leave the table thirsty.

Here's to a long life and a merry one.
A quick death and an easy one.
A pretty girl and an honest one.
A cold beer and another one!

May those who love us love us.
And those that don't love us,
May God turn their hearts.
And if He doesn't turn their hearts,
May he turn their ankles,
So we'll know them by their limping!

Health and a long life to you.
Land without rent to you.
A child every year to you.
And if you can't go to heaven,
May you at least die in Ireland.

# INDEX

**Date:** 4-28-16 **Initial:** HJ
**Damage:** Dirty Edges.